Biscuiteers Book of Iced Biscuits

Harriet Hastings co-founded Biscuiteers with
Stevie Congdon, and is also a co-director of
leading London catering company Lettice.
She is the mother of four young Biscuiteers.

Sarah Moore is a Creative Director, connoisseur
of delicious biscuits, self-confessed vintage
addict and mother of three fine young Biscuiteers.

Biscuiteers Book of Iced Biscuits

Harriet Hastings & Sarah Moore

Photography by Katie Hammond

Kyle Books

This book is very largely thanks to the flair and talent of some very important people:

Victoria Sawdon, book designer, artistic director and talented illustrator who designs and illustrates all Biscuiteers tins.

Sarah Moore, co-author, biscuit designer and creative consultant.

Marion Piffaut, our Production manager who supervised production of the biscuits and generally makes everything happen.

Rina Wanti, Ceridwen Olofson and Belinda Chen, who iced the biscuits for the book.

Katie Hammond, our talented photographer.

Perry Haydn Taylor, Bill Barlow and everyone at Big Fish, our design agency and partners, for all their energy, creativity and brilliance, and for letting us use their studio a lot.

Stevie Congdon, Head of all Biscuiteers production, husband, partner and the fourth Biscuiteer.

Kyle Cathie, Judith Hannam and Vicky Orchard at Kyle Cathie for helping us produce a book we are all really proud of.

And finally to all the other Biscuiteers – our icers, bakers, office staff and, most importantly, customers, who have helped to make it all happen.

First published in Great Britain in 2012 by
Kyle Books
an imprint of Kyle Cathie Limited
23, Howland Street
London W1T 4AY

general.enquiries@kylebooks.com
www.kylebooks.com

ISBN: 978 0 85783 146 0
A CIP catalogue record for this title is available from the British Library

Text © Biscuiteer Baking Company Ltd 2012. www.biscuiteers.com
Design © Kyle Books 2010
Photographs © Katie Hammond 2010 except page 8 © Edward Hill and page 47 © Peter Cassidy

Editor: Vicky Orchard
Design: Victoria Sawdon at Big Fish
Photography: Katie Hammond
Styling: Liz Belton
Food styling: Sarah Moore
Biscuit Production: Marion Piffaut
Copy editor: Clare Hubbard
Production: Gemma John and Nic Jones

Harriet Hastings and Sarah Moore are hereby identified as the authors of this work in accordance with Section 77 of the Copyright, Designs and Patents Act 1988.

Colour reproduction by Scanhouse in Malaysia
Printed in China by C&C Offset Printing Co., Ltd.

Contents

Introduction

We came up with the idea for Biscuiteers on a weekend in New York. We were sure that there were lots of people who are as passionate about biscuits as we are and that there was a real opportunity to set up a biscuit gift business online that was completely different from anything else in the market – biscuits that would look as beautiful as they tasted. In fact, biscuits that people would want to talk about. We thought we could design biscuits unlike anything else on the market – biscuits that would make original, creative presents for everyone.

We started planning Biscuiteers properly in spring of 2007, testing our biscuit recipes in Stevie's catering kitchens. We baked batch after batch to develop our own core flavours – chocolate, vanilla and allspice. From the start we were committed to using the very best natural ingredients to get the flavour we wanted. We then started planning our launch collections, working on our designs and deciding on the big occasions. We wanted the biscuits to be beautiful and witty as, from the start, we saw them as an adult gift. We called them 'collections' because we knew we wanted to launch them seasonally like fashion collections and to keep refreshing and developing the range to ensure our customers kept coming back. It was important that we found our own style – distinctive designs that would make our biscuits instantly recognisable. We created our original biscuits on paper first and then by icing them onto baking paper. There were lots of teething problems! It took

us a while to work out how to dry the icing to the right degree to ensure that the biscuits didn't become soggy. It took us a bit longer to work out how to secure the biscuits in the tins to make sure they didn't arrive broken or chipped.

Biscuiteers launched online in September 2007 with our mission statement 'why send flowers when you can send biscuits instead?'. The media seemed to get it immediately and were very taken with our launch fashion collections which remain some of our bestselling lines. Suddenly we had orders, lots of them. It became apparent that we couldn't continue to camp in Stevie's catering kitchens and office. We moved into our first proper bakery in November 2007.

There was lots of interest in Biscuiteers and we started selling in Selfridges from January 2008 – not just our tin collections but our biscuit cards. We very much wanted to have a simple single biscuit product on the website and came up with the idea of a biscuit greeting card – more than a card but less than a tin. These have really taken off in retail and we now sell in Harrods, Fortnum & Mason, Selfridges and The Conran Shop among others. We also send lots of biscuits overseas. You will find them in Galeries Lafayettes, Colette and La Grande Epicerie in France and as far afield as Dubai and Qatar.

One of the real joys of iced biscuits is their incredible flexibility. Our experienced designers do some wonderful work copying logos and fashion designs and all sorts of products. We have had some exciting commissions, including a collaboration with Anya Hindmarch to create a tin of her handbags and a circus tin exclusively for

Practise: you can practise icing onto sheets of greaseproof paper before you commit to decorating your precious handmade biscuits. Or perhaps buy a packet of biscuits and practise on these until you are more confident; pick ones that are as smooth and level on the top as possible.

Weights and measures: read the recipes and icing guidelines all the way through before you begin. Follow the instructions carefully and make sure that you have accurate scales on which to weigh all your ingredients. Remember: when colouring icing you can always add more colour, but you can't take it away.

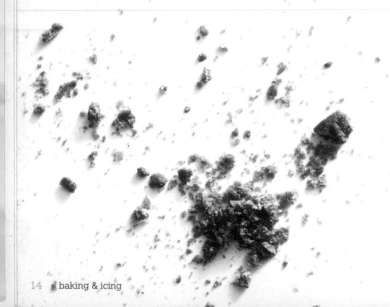

At Biscuiteers we mainly ice our biscuits with royal icing. Traditionally it is made from beating egg whites and icing sugar together for a long time until a thick, smooth, white paste is formed.

Egg whites: lots of recipes use fresh egg whites but we always use a dried egg-white substitute (we use the Meri-White brand) for our biscuits. It is available in most supermarkets and is easier and safer to use than fresh egg whites as it removes the risk of salmonella that can be found in fresh eggs. You can also buy royal icing mix; a pre-mixed combination of icing sugar and dried egg whites that simply needs the right amount of water added to it. Finally, you can also make up the icing using pasteurised liquid egg white. (See Suppliers on page 157 for full details of where these products are available.) Icing made from any of these ingredients tastes pretty much the same, so choose the one that you find easiest or most convenient to prepare.

We use two basic types of royal icing: a thick, smooth paste for piping details and edging, and a runnier glossy mixture for flooding larger areas.

Piping icing: this needs to be smooth and thick, a bit like the texture of toothpaste. It has to be just soft enough to squeeze out of the piping bag, but also thick enough to hold its shape perfectly.

This icing is used for piping borders, which form little 'walls' around the areas of the biscuit that you want to fill with the flooding icing, and for adding fine detail and decoration.

Flooding icing: just about pourable, thicker than double cream, this glossy icing is squeezed onto biscuits to flood areas where a shiny, smooth effect is required. It is well worth investing in a few little squeezy bottles to dispense this icing from. With their screw-on nozzles they are perfect for directing the flow of flooding icing to exactly where it should be.

Remember that making icing is not an exact science. Even though we have a tried-and-tested method of making our icing we often end up adding a little more water or icing sugar to get the icing to exactly the right consistency.

Kit: all icing needs to be made with spotlessly clean and dry equipment, as even tiny amounts of grease can affect how the egg whites whip up and how thick the icing becomes. You can make royal icing by hand but it is much easier if you have an electric whisk or food-processor. If you are making it by hand, combine your chosen ingredients in a mixing bowl and beat for about 10 minutes until you have a lovely bright-white smooth paste.

Additions: adding colour and flavour to the icing affects the consistency, so start with the thickest icing that you need and always add water, colour and flavourings a little at a time.

For best results: you really need to use icing on the day that it is made. Keep it in an airtight container or cover it in the bowl in which it was made as soon as you have transformed it into the type, colour and flavour required. It can be stored in the fridge in piping bags or squeezy bottles for up to three days, but both types of icing separate a little and become less easy to handle on standing for a long time.

Drying biscuits: when you have iced the details, added the baubles and sprinkled on the glitter you might find that the moisture in the icing has affected the crunchiness of the biscuit. At Biscuiteers we return all of our biscuits to the oven at a very low temperature for about 30 minutes to make sure that they are all totally dry. So put them back into an oven set to about 50–70°C/120–160°F/gas mark ½–3 on baking trays to dry off. Smaller biscuits, or ones with just a little iced line detail, won't take very long at all.

Finally: even at Biscuiteers, where we ice and bake all day every day, we still manage to make quite a few biscuits that don't turn out just the way they should. Always aim to make a few more than you need and enjoy the odd imperfect biscuit along the way.

Dough Making

At Biscuiteers we have tried and tested all sorts of recipes in the pursuit of a delicious, easy-to-make and easy-to-use biscuit dough. In this section are our favourite recipes, made from natural ingredients and using real flavours.

In each of the collections we recommend the dough that goes well with the biscuits being made, but these are only suggestions and if you love only the Super Chocolatey variety (see page 34) or you have your own recipe, that's fine too. Whichever one you choose, bear in mind that you need a dough that rolls out easily, cooks evenly and is suitable for cutting. Big chunks of chocolate, whole cranberries or hazelnuts taste delicious but make it difficult to cut and ice evenly.

helpful hints for dough making

* Read through the whole recipe before you start.

* Check that your scales are accurate from time to time (test them with a tin of baked beans or something similar that has a given weight).

* Measure all your ingredients carefully before you begin.

* Take the butter out of the fridge 15–30 minutes (depending on the temperature of your kitchen) before you begin as it will be easier to use.

* When making your dough, try not to handle it any more than you need to as this makes it tough.

* You can make the dough by hand in a big mixing bowl or use a food-processor with the paddle (sometimes called the K-beater) attachment, not the whisk. Remember to start the process on the lowest setting so that the kitchen is not filled with clouds of flour.

* Clear a nice big space on the worktop before rolling and have ready at least two baking trays covered with a sheet of baking parchment for each batch of biscuits to chill and cook on.

Dough Rolling & Keeping

Your dough will be most easy to roll directly after you have made it, as it is naturally softer and more pliable at this point. (If you want to make the dough ahead of time roll it into two flat discs, cover with clingfilm and refrigerate. Bring to room temperature when you need to use it.) Adding flour to help roll out the dough makes it tougher. The trick is to roll it between two sheets of baking parchment. This means you don't have to use any extra flour at all, so this is a technique worth perfecting.

* Divide the dough in two and shape into two flat discs.

* Place the dough on a sheet of parchment.

* To make your dough as even as possible you can use rolling guides; you can buy these from specialist shops. Or improvise by using a couple of wooden spoons.

* Begin by gently squashing the dough down with the rolling pin or your hands, cover with a second sheet of parchment and and then use the rolling pin to roll properly.

* The top sheet of paper may crinkle from time to time, just peel it off and smooth it down gently and start rolling again.

* Gently roll the dough until it is 5mm thick all over.

* Transfer the whole sheet of rolled dough still sandwiched between its sheets of parchment to a baking tray and place in the fridge to chill for at least 20–30 minutes before cutting.

* Repeat the process with the rest of the dough.

cutting, cooking, cooling & keeping

So much time and effort goes into making these biscuits that it is important to look after them carefully at every stage of their production. Keep a close eye on the first couple of batches you cook until you get used to your oven and the recipes.

* Assemble your cutters or templates and start to cut. To use the dough efficiently cut the biscuits out as close together as possible. Lift each biscuit onto the parchment covered baking tray and make sure they are not too close together as the dough will spread a little on baking. Any trimmings can be re-rolled a couple of times.

* Preheat the oven to 170°C/350°F/gas mark 4 before you begin making your biscuits.

* Evenly space the trays in the oven and cook for 14–18 minutes, depending on your oven.

* When the biscuits are evenly cooked and just beginning to turn a golden colour (you can't see this on the Super Chocolatey ones (see page 34) but they begin to darken slightly), remove the trays from the oven and transfer the whole sheet of parchment to a cooling rack or lift each biscuit off with a spatula. Do this carefully as the biscuits will be quite fragile and hot!

* Cool totally before storing or they will lose their crunch, and don't ice the biscuits while they are still warm as the icing will melt.

* Pack the cooked, cooled biscuits between layers of parchment in an airtight tin or plastic container. Store them in a cool, dry place and they will keep for up to a month, iced or un-iced, if you can resist them.

Basic Royal Icing

ingredients:

powdered egg-white recipe

180ml water

1kg icing sugar

30g egg-white powder

all-in-one recipe

150ml cold water

900g royal icing mix

egg-white recipe

4 egg whites (see pack for details of measuring out your egg whites)

900g icing sugar

We use royal icing to ice all of our biscuits. Before you begin, assemble all of the ingredients and colours together that you need to complete your icing. Remember to use spotlessly clean kit and familiarise yourself with the Golden Rules.

* All of the recipes are prepared in the same way. Combine all the ingredients in a mixing bowl, starting with the liquids first.

* Add the dry ingredients and whisk or beat for about 5 minutes if using an electric beater or whisk, or for longer if using a wooden spoon. Whisk slowly to start with to avoid clouds of icing sugar covering you and your kitchen.

* Continue whisking until the ingredients form a thick, smooth paste that is bright white in colour and has the consistency of toothpaste.

* If you are not using immediately, cover the surface of the icing with clingfilm to stop it drying out and refrigerate.

practice makes perfect icing

It can take a while to get used to icing. When we first started, sometimes we would be concentrating so hard on what was coming out of the pointed end of the piping bag, we failed to notice it was all spilling out of the top! And to this day, for every tray of biscuits we make there are always a few that don't make the grade. We have noticed, however, that the biscuits that are misshapen or the ones with the wiggly lines or colourful splodges taste just as good as the perfect ones…

As it takes a lot of time and effort and ingredients to make biscuits, we often introduce our Biscuiteers to icing by placing outlines of the biscuit under sheets of parchment. Like a 'tracing paper' for cooks, parchment can be laid over any design to help you get a feel for icing and you can get a good idea of the pattern and the shape that you want to make on your finished biscuits. Have a look at the iced decorations on page 31 to see what else you can do with parchment.

With most of our designs you need to use a combination of line and flooding icing to create the patterns. The line icing is used to make a little 'wall' around the section of biscuit that you want to fill with the flooding icing, and to add details and decorations to the surface of the biscuit.

When you have filled the icing bags with your chosen colours you are ready to begin.

Preparing & Colouring Icing

Once you have made your basic royal icing, you are now ready to make up your icing palette. This means that you need to prepare the flooding icing and the colours that you're going to need for your chosen biscuits. Check the key on the collection that you are icing, or make up your own colour palette.

At Biscuiteers we use some fantastic powdered colours that are derived from plants. They come in all sorts of colours and are made from carrots and beetroot, spinach and red cabbage, but for home-baking, other options are easier to find.

The traditional bottles of food colouring in most supermarkets are suitable for basic colouring but for a more interesting palette the food-colour gels are really useful and are pretty much essential if you want strong colours, particularly red and black.

Most cookshops stock a range and you can start with a few basic colours and add other colours as you need them.

Most of the biscuits we make use the two types of icing mentioned in the Golden Rules – line and flooding icing (see opposite). For each collection you will usually need about a third of your royal icing mixture to make the line colours and the remaining two-thirds for flooding icing. There are a few exceptions so check the individual collections before you begin. It is worth saving a little plain icing of each texture just in case you need any extra colours or need to make up some more of a particular colour.

Line Icing

* Check to see how many colours of line icing you need and then divide up the icing. Spoon required amounts into clean little bowls (or you can use pots, teacups, mugs, etc.).

* If you are using gel colours, use the tip of a cocktail stick to add a tiny amount of the gel to the icing. Stir the gel into the icing until it is totally mixed in and you see the resulting colour.

* Slowly add more gel, stirring well between additions, until the colour has reached the shade that you need. It is worth taking the colouring process slowly as a little gel colour goes a very long way!

* Cover the surface of the icing with clingfilm and chill each bowl as you make it until you have all the colours that you need for the collection.

Bottled liquid food colouring is a lot less intense than the gels, but you still need to add it gradually a drop at a time. You cannot achieve intense shades with liquid colours, but they work fine for pastel shades. You may need to beat in a little extra icing sugar if the liquid colour begins to thin down your line icing.

You can also try adding your own natural flavours and colours. Whatever you choose, remember that the icing needs to be super smooth and adding any fresh ingredients may affect its setting and keeping qualities. Try coffee; cocoa powder; raspberry, blackcurrant or blackberry purée; lemon or orange zest.

Flooding Icing

The rest of the mixture is used to make flooding icing.

* Place it in a large bowl, gradually add enough water, a few drops at a time, stirring constantly, until you have a smooth, just pourable mixture that has roughly the same consistency as custard.

* Repeat the colouring process with the flooding icing. Look at your designs and count up the number of shades of flooding icing needed. Divide up the mixture, leaving a little spare white icing just in case you need to make any extra later.

* When you have finished, cover the surface of each icing with clingfilm as soon as you have mixed it so that the icing does not start to go hard at the edges, and chill until ready to use.

These are most of the colours that we use and that appear in the collections
top row: grape, eucalyptus, baby blue, Aegean blue, leaf green, sage green, donkey brown
second row: violet, parma violet, grey, deep-sea blue, welly green, pea green, lime green

third row: ivory, hydrangea, strawberry mousse, gentian blue, fuschia, rose, primrose, black
bottom row: white, baby pink, raspberry, red, orange, mustard yellow, bright yellow

Piping Bags & Squeezy Bottles

You are now ready to put your line icing into piping bags, and there are several different types that you can use.

Reusable fabric varieties, also called pastry bags: available from cookshops, these are used with piping nozzles and fittings. You can use them for icing, but be warned: they may take on the colour of the icing you are using; small ones are fine as you normally don't need more than a couple of spoonfuls of each icing.

Paper cones: these are the standard option for most experienced cake decorators. Made from folding a triangle of baking parchment into a perfect cone shape, you can make them at home and use them with or without a nozzle.

Make your own: you can make a simple cone from greaseproof paper. Secure the end with a little sellotape or fold over the top as in the picture below.

Disposable plastic icing bags: at Biscuiteers we use these all the time. You can store your icing in them in the fridge, work with them without having to use piping nozzles and you can instantly see what colour icing is inside.

Nozzles: these are the plastic or metal cones that you put in the end of a piping bag to alter the pattern or type of flow of the icing you are using. They are essential if you are using the reusable fabric variety of piping bag. Normally you push a larger plastic cone inside the bag and then attach your piping nozzle to this from the outside.

For the paper and plastic icing bags you can just snip a tiny triangle off the tip of the bag to create a minuscule hole in the end and make perfect lines without a nozzle. Alternatively, you can snip 1cm or so off the end and use with a nozzle. This is useful if you want to make different types of pattern with the icing, such as ribbons, leaves or star shapes.

Filling an icing bag:

* Choose the type of bag that you want to use and pop in a nozzle (if using).

* Stand the bag upright in a suitable container (jam jar, mug, etc.).

* Carefully spoon the icing into the bag. Use a flexible spatula to scoop up all the icing from the bowl. Don't overfill – you can always refill later.

* When the bag is two-thirds full, pick it up and squeeze the icing down to the bottom of the bag and twist or clip the top shut. (We use those little plastic clips that you can use to keep cereal packets closed, but you can also use elastic bands. Paper cones can be folded shut too).

* If you have not used a nozzle you are now ready to snip the end off the piping bag and begin to ice. Start by cutting the smallest tip off straight across the bag. If you cut at an angle you will create oval lines of icing rather than round. So make sure it is straight!

Squeezy bottles: these are readily available to buy on the Internet or in cake-decorating shops. If you can, buy several of these as using just one will be incredibly time consuming and inconvenient. They come in all different sizes; several small ones are ideal as you are sometimes dealing with quite small quantities of icing. The standard ones come with their own simple nozzle attached. The advantages of these bottles is that they stand upright and the icing does not pour out, you can store the icing in the fridge and it doesn't dry out and they are really helpful in directing just the right amount of icing to just the right place.

* Fill the bottle carefully using a spatula to guide the flow through the wide neck.

* Attach a nozzle to the bottle if it has, one or simply snip off the flexible plastic nozzle to alter the flow of the icing from the bottle.

Icing a line: hold the bag in two hands and gently squeeze the icing down towards the tip of the bag with your top hand and direct its flow with the other hand. * With the tip of the bag just above the surface of the biscuit, but not touching, squeeze evenly and slowly until you create a little trail. Stop squeezing for a second and the trail will stop.

Outlines: if you are making an outline to fill with flooding icing you need to make sure that you join up your trail to form an unbroken wall around the shape you need. If there are any gaps the flooding icing will flow through. When you first start, or if you are icing with children, either choose a larger plain nozzle (No. 3) or cut a larger hole in the end of the bag so that you ice a thicker wall. Let the 'walls' dry for about 5 minutes before filling with flooding icing.

Flooding: at Biscuiteers we squeeze our flooding icing in place using little clear plastic squeezy bottles (see page 27). For very fine details where only a tiny area needs to be flooded it is easier to use a little piping bag. Fill them in just the same way as with line icing (see page 23), but be careful as the icing will pour out of both ends if left unsecured! * For simple designs, or when you are starting out, you can just spoon the icing onto the biscuits and spread it out using a cocktail stick or little skewer. * Remember to return your biscuit to the oven when they are finished – see note on page 15 about drying biscuits.

Flood on flood: this is a delightfully simple and very effective way of decorating. You can make polka dots, stripes, flowers or any design that requires a smooth and glossy pattern. Fill an outline until only just full with flooding icing and immediately ice your patterns onto the surface using more flooding icing. If you initially overfill the biscuit then, when you add the detail, sometimes the icing breaks over the little walls you have made like a burst dam and you end up having to eat the biscuit immediately! Ice the biscuits one at a time so that the background is wet and the details can 'melt' into the surface.

Line on flood: this is perfect for adding detail to your biscuits. Wait until the flooding icing is completely dry and then pipe on the details with line icing.

Glitter and sparkling sugar: there are some styles of biscuit that look just great with a little extra sparkle. There are all sorts of edible glitters on the market to help you add that special twinkle. As a general rule, less is more! Remember that the glitter and sugar will stick to any icing that is still wet. So either allow the biscuit to dry completely and then pipe on a line where you want the glitter, or just ice and add glitter to the area to be glittered first, then add everything else around it. Either way, the wetter the icing is, the more glitter will stick to it.

Baubles and sugar decorations: whenever you want to add ready-made decorations to your biscuits you need to either drop and gently press them onto wet the icing or, if the area you want to add them to has already set, just squeeze on a tiny dot of line icing to use as a spot of 'glue'.

Writing: for fine details and writing use line icing in your chosen colour and make sure that you have either cut the tiniest tip off the piping bag for a fine line, or that you use a fine plain piping nozzle (No. 1). If you struggle to squeeze all the text or letters onto your biscuit, try writing out the message or name to the correct scale on a computer, print it out and then cover this with baking parchment to practise icing over the top. For larger biscuits or individual letters you can use flooding icing for thicker, smoother letters.

Dusts and shimmers: these are really fine edible glittery powders that can be rubbed or painted onto the iced biscuit, a little like using make-up! They are used just on the surface and are really useful for adding a metallic sheen or pearlised look.

Icing a dot: hold the piping bag just above the surface where you want to make a little dot. Squeeze until you have the size of dot required, gently lifting as you go. Stop squeezing and then remove the piping bag.

Using nozzles: there is a large variety of piping nozzles and tubes in cookshops and cake-decorating shops. The different shapes create different icing trails as the icing is squeezed out. A star nozzle is great for little rosettes and there are flat versions that are really useful for piping ribbons. Most of the effects that can be produced with a nozzle can be achieved with a disposable or paper piping bag too. Cut across the end at an angle for icing trails with a flatter or oval-shaped profile. Cutting a tiny 'v' instead of straight across produces a trail that is great for icing leaves. So buy a small selection of nozzles or experiment with cutting piping bags.

Making your own embellishments: if you have any leftover line icing, use it to make your own decorative embellishments. Pipe shapes onto parchment. Try little flowers or a lacy butterfly wing, initials or little animals. Either let them totally dry out naturally, or pop them into the drying oven for 30 minutes (see page 15). Finely detailed shapes are very fragile when dry and need to be peeled off carefully. If they are totally dry these shapes can be kept for at least a month in an airtight container. You can use them to decorate cupcakes too.

Plain Biscuit Recipe

You can use this dough as a base for making all sorts of other flavours of biscuit. Have a look at the following pages for some variations, as well as those listed below.

ingredients

makes 24 biscuits

350g plain flour

100g self raising flour

125g granulated sugar

125g salted butter, diced

125g golden syrup

1 large egg, lightly beaten

basic recipe

* Sift the flours together into a mixing bowl, add the sugar and mix well.

* Add the butter. Using just the tips of your fingers, rub together the ingredients until the mixture resembles fine breadcrumbs.

* When all the butter is evenly mixed in, make a well in the centre and add the syrup and the egg.

* Mix well, drawing in any of the flour left at the sides of the bowl and stop as soon as a ball has formed.

* Place the dough onto your clean worktop. Divide into two and squash the dough into two even-sized flat discs. Cover and chill until ready to use, or roll out immediately (see pages 18–19).

* For cutting, cooking, cooling and keeping, follow the instructions on page 19.

variations on the theme

If there are some ingredients you want to experiment with, there are a couple of things to consider. If you are making dough for biscuits that are to be rolled, cut and iced, then you don't want to add massive chunks of chocolate or hazelnut or whatever it is you have in mind, as they make the process quite tricky. So cut, break or crunch up your ingredients into very small pieces before you use them. Add all dry ingredients to the flour and sugar and any liquid ingredients mixed in with the egg.

Nutmeg: add ½ tablespoon of grated nutmeg.

Ginger: add 1 tablespoon of ground ginger, and some finely diced crystallised ginger if you like.

Lemon: add the grated zest of two lemons.

Orange: add the grated zest of two oranges and little orange-flavoured chocolate chunks.

Cinnamon and orange: add the grated zest of two oranges and ½ tablespoon of cinnamon.

Coffee: add 3 tablespoons of instant coffee dissolved in 1 tablespoon of water.

Cardamom: crush 8 dried cardamom pods and add the little dried seeds from inside the husks.

Super Chocolatey Biscuits

This is a classic Biscuiteers' recipe. The biscuits have a slightly doughy texture and the rich, bitter chocolateyness works beautifully with the sweet icing.

ingredients

makes 24 biscuits

275g plain flour

100g self raising flour

75g good quality cocoa powder

125g granulated sugar

125g salted butter, diced

125g golden syrup

1 large egg, lightly beaten

basic recipe

* Sift the flours and cocoa together into a mixing bowl, add the sugar and mix well.

* Add the butter. Using just the tips of your fingers, rub together the ingredients until the mixture resembles fine breadcrumbs.

* When all the butter is evenly mixed in, make a well in the centre and add the syrup and the egg.

* Mix well, drawing in any of the flour left at the sides of the bowl and stop as soon as a ball has formed.

* Place the dough onto your clean worktop. Divide into two and squash the dough into two even-sized flat discs. Cover and chill until ready to use, or roll out immediately (see pages 18–19).

* For cutting, cooking, cooling and keeping, follow the instructions on page 19.

variations on the theme

Orange: chocolate and orange is a time-honoured flavour combination that works beautifully. Grate the zest of two medium oranges on the finest area of a grater. Stir the zest evenly into the beaten egg mixture and then follow the basic recipe. You can also add little chunks of orange-flavoured chocolate to the mixture too.

Vanilla Biscuits

Natural vanilla has a delicious taste that is perfect for adding to biscuits. At Biscuiteers we only use the whole pods of Madagascan vanilla for the finest flavour. You can also use good-quality natural vanilla essence or, at a pinch, vanilla flavouring.

ingredients

makes 24 biscuits

½ of vanilla pods or
½ teaspoon natural
vanilla essence

350g plain flour

100g self raising flour

125g granulated sugar

125g salted butter, diced

125g golden syrup

1 large egg, lightly beaten

* If you are using the whole vanilla pod, slice down the pod with a sharp knife so that it splits in two. Scrape the tiny black seeds from the pod with a teaspoon and add to the sugar. If you are using vanilla essence, add to the lightly beaten egg.

* Sift the flours together into a mixing bowl, add the sugar and mix well.

* Add the butter. Using just the tips of your fingers, rub together the ingredients until the mixture resembles fine breadcrumbs.

* When all the butter is evenly mixed in, make a well in the centre and add the syrup and the egg.

* Place the dough onto your clean worktop. Divide into two and squash the dough into two even-sized flat discs. Cover and chill until ready to use, or roll out immediately (see pages 18–19).

* For cutting, cooking, cooling and keeping, follow the instructions on page 19.

Tip: you can pop the deseeded vanilla pod into a bag of sugar to make vanilla-scented sugar to use in your next batch of biscuits.

Coconut Biscuits

This recipe produces a delicate coconut-flavoured biscuit that has a slightly crunchier texture than the other recipes.

ingredients

makes 24 biscuits

350g plain flour

100g self raising flour

125g granulated sugar

75g desiccated coconut

125g salted butter, diced

125g golden syrup

1 large egg, lightly beaten

* Sift the flours together into a mixing bowl, add the sugar and desiccated coconut and mix well.

* Add the butter. Using just the tips of your fingers, rub together the ingredients until the mixture resembles fine breadcrumbs.

* When all the butter is evenly mixed in, make a well in the centre and add the syrup and the egg.

* Mix well, drawing in any of the flour left at the sides of the bowl and stop as soon as a ball has formed.

* Place the dough onto your clean worktop. Divide into two and squash the dough into two even-sized flat discs. Cover and chill until ready to use, or roll out immediately (see pages 18–19).

* For cutting, cooking, cooling and keeping, follow the instructions on page 19.

Simple Butter Biscuits

These lovely shortbread-style biscuits have a satisfying buttery taste and are really good for the Bake with Mother collection (see pages 136–139). They are slightly more fragile and crumbly than the other biscuits, so they're not ideal if you've got to transport them very far.

ingredients

makes approx. 30 biscuits

500g plain flour

180g caster sugar

250g salted butter, diced

2 large eggs, lightly beaten

splash of milk, if required

* Sift the flour and sugar together into a mixing bowl and mix well.

* Add the butter. Using just the tips of your fingers, rub together the ingredients until the mixture resembles fine breadcrumbs.

* When all the butter is evenly mixed in, make a well in the centre and add the eggs and a splash of milk, if required, to bring it all together into a smooth dough.

* Place the dough onto your clean worktop. Divide into two and squash the dough into two even-sized flat discs. Cover and chill until ready to use, or roll out immediately (see pages 18–19).

* For cutting, cooking, cooling and keeping, follow the instructions on page 19.

Almond / Hazelnut Biscuits

These biscuits are lovely served alongside fruity puddings. Their delicate nutty flavour makes them great to enjoy un-iced too.

ingredients

makes 24 biscuits

350g plain flour

125g granulated sugar

125g salted butter, diced

125g golden syrup

1 large egg, lightly beaten

100g ground almonds
or 1 teaspoon of
almond essence

or 100g hazelnuts,
toasted and chopped

* Sift the flour into a mixing bowl, add the sugar and mix well.

* Add the butter. Using just the tips of your fingers, rub together the ingredients until the mixture resembles fine breadcrumbs.

* When all the butter is evenly mixed in, add the almonds or hazelnuts and stir in evenly.

* Make a well in the centre and add the syrup and the egg, and the almond essence if using.

* Mix well, drawing in any of the flour left at the side of the bowl and stop as soon as a ball has formed.

* Place the dough onto your clean worktop. Divide into two and squash the dough into two even-sized flat discs. Cover and chill until ready to use, or roll out immediately (see pages 18–19).

* For cutting, cooking, cooling and keeping, follow the instructions on page 19.

Gluten-free Chocolate Biscuits

The texture of these biscuits is certainly more shortbready than our usual biscuit recipes. These biscuits need to be fully dried as their crumbly texture makes them liable to going a little soft when the icing is piped on. You also need to ensure that the icing colours and ingredients are gluten free.

ingredients

makes 24 biscuits

250g gluten-free flour

pinch salt

100g sugar

100g butter

100g dark chocolate

* Sift all the dry ingredients into a bowl and mix together.

* Melt chocolate and butter together carefully over a low heat and pour into the dry ingredients.

* Stir well and then using just the tips of your fingers, rub together the ingredients until the mixture comes together. Stop as soon as a ball can be formed.

* Place the dough onto your clean worktop. Divide into two and squash the dough into two even-sized flat discs. Cover and chill until ready to use, or roll out immediately (see pages 18–19).

* For cutting, cooking, cooling and keeping, follow the instructions on page 19.

Anzac Biscuits

These Australian classics have a mixture of oats and coconut to thank for their lovely crunchy texture. Dry them out carefully when they have been iced to keep their delicate, crumbly texture.

ingredients

makes 24 biscuits

250g plain flour

100g desiccated coconut

½ teaspoon baking powder

100g fine porridge oats

150g caster sugar

175g butter, diced

1 tablespoon golden syrup

1 large egg, lightly beaten

* Sift the flour and baking powder together into a mixing bowl.

* Stir in the coconut, oats and sugar.

* Add the butter. Using just the tips of your fingers, rub together the ingredients until the mixture resembles fine breadcrumbs.

* When all the butter is evenly mixed in, make a well in the centre and add the syrup and the egg.

* Mix well, drawing in any of the flour left at the sides of the bowl and stop as soon as a ball has formed.

* Place the dough onto your clean worktop. Divide into two and squash the dough into two even-sized flat discs. Cover and chill until ready to use, or roll out immediately (see pages 18–19).

* For cutting, cooking, cooling and keeping, follow the instructions on page 19.

Peanut Butter Biscuits

We love the savoury flavour that the peanuts bring to this recipe. You can use crunchy or smooth peanut butter, depending on what is in your cupboard. The crunchy one does have a lovely texture though. Be sure to let everyone know that these biscuits contain peanuts, as some people are allergic to them.

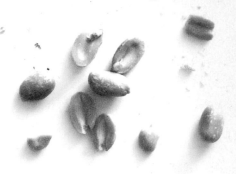

ingredients

makes 24 biscuits

250g plain flour

100g soft brown sugar

½ teaspoon baking powder

65g salted butter, diced

65g golden syrup

1 egg, lightly beaten

1-2 tablespoons milk

65g peanut butter

* Sift the flour, sugar and baking powder into a mixing bowl and mix well.

* Add the butter. Using just the tips of your fingers, rub together the ingredients until the mixture resembles fine breadcrumbs.

* In a separate bowl, mix together the egg, syrup, one tablespoon of milk and the peanut butter.

* Make a well in the centre of the dry ingredients and add the liquid mixture. Bring it all together to form a soft dough. Add a dash more milk if required.

* Place the dough onto your clean worktop. Divide into two and squash the dough into two even-sized flat discs. Cover and chill until ready to use, or roll out immediately (see pages 18–19).

* For cutting, cooking, cooling and keeping, follow the instructions on page 19.

Treacle Spice Biscuits

This is a lovely recipe that is perfect for making bauble-shaped biscuits to hang on the Christmas tree or gingerbread men.

ingredients

makes 24 biscuits

200g plain flour

½ teaspoon baking powder

½ teaspoons ground ginger

¼ teaspoon cinnamon

½ teaspoon mixed spice

50g muscovado dark brown sugar

100g salted butter, diced

50g black treacle or molasses

* Sift the flour, baking powder and all the spices into a mixing bowl. Add the sugar and mix well.

* Add the butter. Using just the tips of your fingers, rub together the ingredients until the mixture resembles fine breadcrumbs.

* When all the butter is evenly mixed in, make a well in the centre and add the treacle and bring it all together. You will know when it is all mixed in as it will have an even colour all over with not too many streaks of treacle.

* Place the dough onto your clean worktop. Divide into two and squash the dough into two even-sized flat discs. Cover and chill until ready to use, or roll out immediately (see pages 18–19).

* For cooking, cooling and keeping follow the instructions on page 19.

Traditional Advent

This collection is just one more excuse to ice some biscuits at Christmas. Have a look at all the traditional Christmas images that you can find and use them as inspiration for your twenty four advent biscuits. Add sparkles and glitter, snowflakes and tiny shiny baubles, gold leaf or shimmering dust. Hide each biscuit in a tiny stocking, wrap them in squares of festive paper or sew yourself a keepsake calendar like the one here.

Iced Christmas

Everyone loves this sparkling Christmas collection. Simple and jolly, this has appeal for all the family. White gift-tag biscuits iced with Christmas messages and the names of your nearest and dearest make great place settings on Christmas day too.

cutters

tree
snowman
reindeer
sleigh
stocking

recipes

1 quantity cinnamon-and-orange-flavoured Plain Biscuit dough (see page 33); makes 2 stockings, 3 reindeer, 1 sleigh, 2 snowmen and 1 large Christmas tree

1 quantity Basic Royal Icing (see page 21)

line icing

welly green
red
white
black
donkey brown

flooding icing

baby blue
white

embellishments

silver and gold baubles
silver sparkly glitter sugar

Christmas tree

Ice trunk with donkey brown line icing. * Use welly green line icing to add boughs. Start at the top and work down to base. Allow to dry for at least 5 minutes. * Use white runny icing to add 'snow' on the tips of all the branches and sprinkle with silver glitter before it dries. * Drop on tiny silver and gold baubles and any other embellishments you want to add.

Rudolph and friends

Carefully outline head, body and legs in white. Allow to dry for at least 5 minutes. * Flood with white. Allow to dry. * Add ears in white, eye in black and red nose. * Ice antlers in fine donkey brown line and a bow if you wish in any colour.

snowflake

Pipe the outline in white and leave to dry. * Flood with white runny icing and, when dry, use more white line and glitter if you wish to add flake details.

snowman

Ice all of the hat using black line icing. * Use white line icing to outline head and body. Allow to dry for at least 5 minutes. * Flood with white. Pop all the little air bubbles that form with a cocktail stick if you want a perfect finish. Allow to dry. * Pipe on the scarf in colour of your choice. Finish with a little red radish nose, eyes and some black buttons. * You could also add a sprig of holly or a robin to the hat.

stocking

Outline in white and allow to dry for at least 5 minutes. * Flood the middle with white and allow to dry until totally set. * Ice on little spots where you want glitter. Sprinkle on glitter and carefully shake off excess. * Make outline for presents in any colour, allow to dry and fill with flooding icing. Allow to dry. * Pipe on ribbons and bows and your chosen pattern on the stocking.

sleigh

Outline the sleigh in red line. Allow to dry for at least 5 minutes. * Flood with baby blue flooding icing. Allow to dry until totally set. * Ice on little spots of white where you want frosting to be. Sprinkle on silver glitter before spots dry; carefully shake off excess. * Add runners and swirls in red line.

Christmas Baubles.

Making biscuits at Christmas time is great: you can give them as presents, use them as decoration, advent treats or even as place names on the Christmas table. These baubles are specially designed to hang on your tree and they each have a little hole at the top to thread through with pretty ribbon. They can even be iced on both sides: just let the first side dry totally before icing on the reverse.

kit

bauble cutters, or you can just use some basic round and fluted cutters in different sizes
wide drinking straws
pretty ribbon or thread

recipes

1 quantity cinnamon-and-orange flavoured Plain Biscuit dough (see page 33) or Treacle Spice Biscuits dough (see page 39) aim to make 3/4 of each bauble

1 quantity Basic Royal Icing (see page 21)

line icing

white
baby pink
fuschia
red
parma violet
lime green
welly green

flooding icing

white
baby pink
fuschia
red

embellishments

gold and silver balls
sugar snowflakes
glitter sugar in pink

Helpful hints: roll and cut your biscuits as per the dough instructions, but remember to cut a hole at the top of each biscuit with the end of a drinking straw BEFORE baking. Remember to ice AROUND each hole so you can easily thread through with ribbon.

trellis bauble

Outline the bauble in parma violet line, add pink line tassel and fuschia detail around the ribbon hole. * When dry, flood the circle with red and wait for a minute to let it set. * Pipe the criss-cross pattern in parma violet line. * Add the dots of lime green icing and the little golden baubles to decorate.

teardrop bauble

This is all iced in line icing. * Use your own favourite colours. * Separating each band with a green stripe, ice all the way down in coloured bands. * Drop gold and silver balls onto the decoration whilst the icing is still wet.

candy cane

Pipe around the outline and the hole in pink line and allow to dry. * Flood with white runny icing, remove air bubbles with a cocktail stick and leave to set. * Ice the candy stripes in alternate baby pink and lime green lines.

spinning top bauble

Outline the bauble in lime green line icing. Flood the middle with baby pink runny icing and allow to set. * Pipe around the ribbon hole in fuschia and then add the lines of lime green across the bauble. * Add zigzag detail in welly green and use fuschia for the little polka dots.

swedish jumper bauble

Ice outline in lime green line icing and pipe red around the ribbon hole. * Flood the middle with fuschia flooding icing and allow to set. * Add lime green and welly green for the zigzags and polka dots. * Drop sugar snowflakes onto the icing whilst it is still wet.

gingerbread House

There are whole cutter kits just for making these houses, but it is really easy just to make a paper version and cut around it using a clean ruler. Then you can choose the size of your house, add porches, chimneys, dormer windows or whatever you fancy.

cutters

gingerbread man
Christmas tree
gingerbread house cutter set
(or cut freehand)

recipes

2 quantities ginger flavoured Plain Biscuit dough or treacle spiced dough (see page 33); makes 1 Father Ginger, 1 large house and a small glade of trees

2 quantities Basic Royal Icing (see page 21)

line icing

red
white
leaf green
eucalyptus
brown

flooding icing

white
colours of your choice
for candy drops
black

embellishments

sparkly sugar

gingerbread house

You will need to make the front and back gables of the house first and then carefully measure two large roof rectangles and then two smaller wall sections to scale. Use suitable heart, square and rectangle cutters or the point of a knife to make the cut out areas. Save any squares to make a chimney too. And just in case a panel breaks you can glue it back together using line icing.

Assemble the walls of the house first using lots of thick line icing. You may want to support it with books or a bag of flour until the icing sets. Then add the two roof panels and a chimney on top if you like, again using plenty of icing and leave the whole thing to set.

To ice the house place it onto a sheet of parchment then begin to decorate. Decide on your pattern and ice directly onto the house. * Use white line to make the snowy roof and snowdrifts and when it has dried add icicles too.

You can make candy canes and little coloured spots in the same way as the cake decorations on page 79 and glue them on with white line icing. * When you have finished icing and everything is totally dry you can pipe on detail in white line icing and cover with sparkly sugar. * Tap off the excess and wait for Christmas.

Christmas tree

Pipe on branches in various green line icing. * When totally dry, add snow in white line icing to the end of the branches and sprinkle with sparkly sugar. * Tap off excess.

Father Ginger

Outline the boots and belt in black line and dry before flooding in black runny icing. * Add red line around arms and legs and hat and yellow line buckle detail. * Add plenty of white line icing to beard, gloves and trims and finish with a brown line smile and eyes.

Easter Eggs

Fabergé darling? We have taken our inspiration for our largest eggs from Fabergé's most precious of Easter offerings. Eggs of easter past have influenced our other patterns that are full of pretty spots, dots and braids. Make up your own designs, in your favourite colours or ice the smallest ovals like little speckled songbird eggs.

cutters

3 different-sized egg cutters

recipes

1 quantity Super Chocolately Biscuits dough (see page 34); makes 5 large, 7 medium and 10 small eggs

1 quantity Basic Royal Icing (see page 21)

line icing

Aegean blue
fuschia
white
pea green
deep baby pink

flooding icing

baby pink
Aegean blue
fuschia

embellishments

gold and silver baubles
gold and silver glitter sugar

Fabergé sparkler

Pipe outline of the largest egg in fuschia and dry for 5 minutes. * Flood with baby pink runny icing and allow to dry. * When set add the jewel outline, all the swirls, dots and lines that you want to make your pattern in pea green line. * When everything is totally dry, flood the centre of the jewel in baby blue flooding icing and sprinkle with silver glitter sugar. * Finally add any glittering baubles using line icing as glue.

all wrapped up egg

Pipe outline of the smallest egg in fuschia and dry for 5 minutes. * Flood with baby pink flooding icing and allow to dry. * Use your favourite colours of line icing, (we use Aegean blue, pea green, white and fuschia here) to add spots, ric-rac, that old fashoined wavy ribbon, and lines for the perfect pretty pattern.

dotty egg

Outline the egg in fushcia line and leave to dry for five minutes. * Just fill the centre of egg with flooding fushia icing (don't overfill or it will overflow when the dots are added) and immediately add spots of flooding icing to make the dotty pattern, before the icing has had a chance to set.

Tips: if you would like to use your beautiful bejewelled biscuits to decorate an Easter tree, cut a hole with the end of a drinking straw in the top of each egg before you bake the biscuits. Thread pretty ribbon through the hole after the biscuits have been iced and dried.

Joys of Spring

We love the kissing bunnies and the little lambs and the all-round freshness of this sweet springtime collection. There are a whole host of suitable cutters available – you'll be spoilt for choice!

cutters

lamb
chick
bunny
egg
primroses

recipes

1 quantity Super Chocolately Biscuits dough (see page 31); makes around 20 if you make lots of little eggs too

1 quantity Basic Royal Icing (see page 21)

line icing

black
white
welly green (tiny amount)
baby blue
baby pink
bright yellow
primrose

flooding icing

donkey brown
white
Aegean blue
primrose
bright yellow

lamb

Use either black or white line icing to ice fluffy balls of wool all over. Allow to dry for 5 minutes. * Add eyes in black and a nose in baby pink.

bunny

Use whichever colour you like to outline the bunny shape. * Allow to dry for 5 minutes and then flood the whole of the bunny in runny icing of the same colour. * When this has set add a fluffy tail and ear details in white line. * Add a ribbon in a contrasting line colour and, finally, add the eye with a tiny spot of black line. and baby pink for the nose.

egg

Ice the outline first in either blue or brown line. Allow to dry for 5 minutes. * Flood with blue or brown and immediately add a few contrasting blue or brown dots. * Muddle them into background to create speckled effect using the tip of a cocktail stick.

chick

Outline chick in yellow line. Allow to dry for 5 minutes. * Flood with yellow. Allow to dry. * Add wing and feather details in yellow line. * Add a beak in baby pink line and an eye in black.

primroses

Use a primrose yellow line to pipe outline round flowers. Allow to dry for 5 minutes. * Flood the flower with primrose yellow. Allow to dry. * Pipe bright yellow centres in the flowers.

Mother's Day

This is the sewing basket that no mother should be without as it is packed with all the essentials. Find a little basket and line it with pretty material or tissue paper and place the biscuits inside. A lovely gift for Mum.

cutters

scissors
thimble
strawberry pin cushion
large round cutter for
balls of wool
tiny round cutter for buttons
rectangles for needles
and cotton reels

recipes

1 quantity Treacle Spice
Biscuits dough (see page 39);
makes approx. 19 biscuits

1 quantity Basic Royal Icing
(see page 21)

line icing

red
baby pink
Aegean blue
welly green
primrose
white
ivory

flooding icing

Aegean blue
red
white
ivory

needles

Ice a scalloped outline in white
and allow to dry for about 5 minutes.
* Fill with baby blue flooding icing
and allow to set. * Use line icing to
add flower pattern * Add the needles
in white and thread in red.

cotton reels

Pipe the thread on reel in line icing of
your choice. * Add outline of wooden
spool in white line and allow to dry for
5 minutes. * Flood this area with white
and allow to set. * Add details to spool
in any colour line icing.

balls of wool

Using just line icing, in any colour,
pipe on fine lines in the pattern of
a ball of wool.

thimble

Using line icing, pipe on the pattern
of the thimble.

scissors

Ice handles in ivory outline. * Use
Aegean blue to outline the blades
and allow to dry for 5 minutes. * Flood
the blades with white and the handles
in ivory and allow to set. * Add details
to blades with Aegean blue line icing.

buttons

Ice around the outline and the holes
in your chosen line colour and allow
to dry for 5 minutes. * Flood with a
different colour and allow to set. * Add
any details to the buttons with line icing.

strawberry pincushion

Ice little leaves and stalk on top of
the strawberry in green line. * Ice
strawberry in red line in a wiggly
'knitted' pattern, and add flowers and
ribbon in line icing too. Allow to dry.
* Pipe little white pins and finish off
with dots of colour on ends.

Father's Day

This is one toolkit that Dad will really enjoy getting out. You can make this collection as elaborate or simple as you like. Add some power tools and goggles or just make lots of paintbrushes with different 'paint' on the ends.

cutters

snippers
spanners
pliers
hammer
saw
screwdriver
paintbrush

recipes

Use your Father's favourite biscuit dough

1 quantity Basic Royal Icing (see page 21)

line icing

bright yellow
grey
black
red
add more colours for different paints on the brushes if you like

flooding icing

bright yellow
grey
black
red

embellishments

silver glitter or lustre dust, if liked

pliers

Pipe the outline of handles in red line and the jaws of the pliers in grey. Remember to leave little hole. Allow to dry for 5 minutes. * Flood handles in red and jaws in grey. * Add detail with grey line.

saw

Outline handle in yellow line and the blade in grey. Allow to dry for 5 minutes. * Flood the handle with yellow and the blade with grey.

paintbrush

Outline the handle in yellow line and the bit that holds the bristles in grey. Allow to dry. * Flood the handle with yellow and the bristle holder with grey. * Pipe the bristles in black line. Allow to dry. * Using flooding icing, carefully squeeze the 'paint' onto the bristles.

hammer

Pipe around head of hammer with grey line. Outline handle in black. Allow to dry for 5 minutes. * Flood handle with black and head with grey. Allow to dry. * Add stripe detail in red line on handle.

screwdriver

Outline the handle in yellow line and the screwdriver in grey. Allow to dry for 5 minutes. * Flood the handle with yellow and the screwdriver with grey. * Add the handle detail in black line.

spanners and snippers

Ice around the outline in grey line. Allow to dry for 5 minutes. * Flood with grey icing. * Add details in black line if you wish.

Witch's Spell

We love the idea of spells and cauldrons so here are all the ingredients for a truly terrifying witches' brew, to be cast under the watchful eyes of the owl and the black cat. Spells still work just as well with only a couple of ingredients, so choose your favourites from our collection.

cutters

pumpkin
cat
ghost
snake
mouse
bat
witch
newt

recipes

1 quantity Treacle Spice Biscuits dough (see page 39); makes at least 16, add more snakes and mice to use up any spare dough

1 quantity Basic Royal Icing (see page 21)

line icing

black
orange
welly green
bright yellow
donkey brown
grey
white

flooding icing

grey
welly green
orange
white
black

embellishments

silver and red glitter

pumpkin

Use green line to make stalk detail. Pipe orange line around edge of pumpkin and add eye and mouth details. Allow to dry for 5 minutes. * Flood with orange. Allow to dry. * Add orange lines for stripes to finish, if wished.

little ghost

Outline the body of ghost in white. Outline the eyes and mouth in orange. Allow to dry for 5 minutes. * Flood with white runny icing and allow to dry.

big bat

Ice around wing outline in black and pipe a little oval line for the tummy. Allow to dry for 5 minutes. * Flood the wings and head with black. After 1 minute, sprinkle on silver glitter and flood the tummy with black. Allow to dry. * Brush off excess glitter and add two yellow eyes.

snake

Outline in green. Allow to dry for 5 minutes. * Flood with green. Before it has a chance to set, pipe on tiny yellow spots. Allow to dry. * Pipe on nose and eye details.

newt

Ice around outline of body in green line and add little feet. Allow to dry. * Flood body in green and pipe on tiny yellow or orange spots before green icing sets. * Add little white eyes with black pupils.

witch

Ice around witch's cloak, hair and hat in black and face in green line. Allow to dry for 5 minutes. * Flood whole of witch's cloak, hair and hat in black and allow to dry. * Pipe broom with brown line and add stockings in striped line and dry. * Pipe little orange shoes and cover in sparkling red glitter.

cat

Outline in black line. Allow to dry for 5 minutes. * Flood the centre with black and allow to dry. * Add a bright yellow collar and black and orange eye.

Note: some black colours stain mouths and teeth; settle for a charcoal grey if you don't want black fangs.

mini mouse

Outline the body of mouse in grey. Allow to dry for 5 minutes. * Flood with grey. Allow to dry. * Use fine black line to add eye, nose and ear details and little paws.

Chanukah

This is a very simple-to-ice collection in celebration of Chanukah. We have used the traditional colour palette to ice all the shapes. We think that you might find these biscuits go down very well at any one of the eight festival nights. Take some of the biscuit ideas to use as favours at bar mitzvahs or bat mitzvahs too.

cutters

Star of David
money
menorah
dreidel
Torah

recipes

1 quantity lemon flavoured Plain Biscuit dough (see page 33); makes approx. 15 biscuits

1 quantity Basic Royal Icing (see page 21)

line icing

bright yellow (tiny amount)
baby blue
white
gentian blue

flooding icing

baby blue
white
gentian blue

embellishments

silver glitter

Star of David and dreidel

Ice the outline and flood all in white. * Dry and then add details in gentian line. Add silver glitter before the line dries if you wish.

Menorah

Outline and flood in gentian blue and leave to set. * Ice on the candles in white and finish with yellow line-icing flames.

polka dot gift

Pipe the outline in gentian blue line icing and leave to set. * Flood until just full with white runny icing and then immediately squeeze on spots of gentian blue runny icing. * Leave to set, then add the ribbon and bow detail in gentian blue line.

star gift

Pipe on outline of the shape of the gift in baby blue. * Leave to set and then flood with gentian blue, white or baby blue runny icing. When dry, pipe on the ribbon and bow details in contrasting line icing.

little present

Ice smaller versions of the presents detailed above.

Thanksgiving

This is the Biscuiteers' homage to all good things at Thanksgiving. You can ice similar selections to celebrate harvest too.

cutters

leaves
acorn
pumpkin
turkey
apple

recipes

1 quantity cinnamon-and-orange-flavoured Plain Biscuit dough (see page 33); makes at least 20 if you use small leaf cutters

1 quantity Basic Royal Icing (see page 21)

line icing

orange
red
bright yellow
eucalyptus
pea green
donkey brown

flooding icing

bright yellow
lime green
pea green
donkey brown
red
eucalyptus
orange

pumpkin

Use pea green line to add stalk detail at top. * Pipe orange line all around edge. Allow to dry for 5 minutes. * Flood with orange icing. Allow to set. * Add orange lines for the stripes on pumpkin.

leaves

All leaves are iced in same way. Outline and allow to dry for 5 minutes. * Flood. Don't make it too full if you want to add spots and colours. Add these before the first layer sets. Allow to dry. * Ice on vein details.

turkey

Use line icing to pipe feathers and details on turkey. Start at beak and gradually add feathers all way down in brown, orange, red and eucalyptus. * Add little donkey brown feet too.

acorn

Ice cup with donkey brown line criss-cross pattern. Outline around acorn in eucalyptus. Allow to dry for 5 minutes. * Flood acorn with same eucalyptus icing.

apple

Pipe around outline of apple in red. Add stalk in brown and leaf in pea green line. Allow to dry for 5 minutes. * Flood apple with red runny icing.

The Happy Couple

At Biscuiteers we have a lot of fun designing our Jolly Gingers. Here are some of our ginger love collection, but you can ice cakes, Easter eggs, hammers or hearts into their hands for occasions throughout the year. We mainly use line icing for decorating them as they are quite big biscuits.

cutters

Biscuiteers gingerbread cutter

recipes

1 quantity ginger flavoured Plain Biscuit dough (see page 33); makes 8–10 big gingers

1 quantity Basic Royal Icing (see page 21)

line icing

fuchsia
white
donkey brown
red
bright yellow
pea green
baby blue
selection of colours for flowers

embellishments

silver glitter sugar

bride

Use a fine line icing and pipe veil, dress, shoes and gloves in white.
* Add brown arm and eye details, pink lips, headdress in bright yellow and a bunch of flowers all in line icing.
* Leave to dry completely. * Add more white line icing and shake on glitter sugar for any areas you would like to sparkle.

ginger bunch

Ice collar and arms in white line.
* Add donkey brown hands.
* Pipe pea green stems and leaves and then ice the flowers in your favourite pretty colours.

groom

Add donkey brown arm, eyes and mouth in line icing. * Pipe outline of box and add bow tie in red. Ice inside box and add detail to bow tie in fuchsia.
* Pipe ring in bright yellow line icing and leave until all completely dry. * Add white line highlight to diamond and ring, sprinkle with glitter sugar and tap off excess.

Love Hearts

These hearts are deceptively simple to ice and suitable for all sorts of occasions. The glossy icing and bright colours make them one of our favourites. For extra fine patterns place runny icing into a piping bag to add the pattern detail.

cutters

hearts

recipes

1 quantity Super Chocolatey Biscuits dough (see page 34); makes 16–18 love hearts

1 quantity Basic Royal Icing (see page 21)

line icing

Aegean blue
orange
rose
lime green

flooding icing

orange
Aegean blue
raspberry
white

All of the hearts are iced in the same way. Outline the heart shape with line icing and leave to dry. * Flood, but do not to overfill, each one in a contrasting colour. * Before it has a chance to set, pipe or squeeze on stripes or dots of more runny icing in various colours. * Then, using the tip of a cocktail stick, drag up and down through the lines to ripple the pattern. * Clean the cocktail stick between each stroke to keep the pattern neat.

New Baby

This is the sweetest little collection to celebrate a new baby. Think light pastel shades when it comes to mixing your colours, and don't feel that you have to do all three different shades. A row of little ducks all one colour looks just as good, and they are all delightfully simple to ice too. Make the line icing a couple of shades darker than the flooding icing.

cutters

mummy and baby duck

recipes

1 quantity Simple Butter Biscuits dough (see page 37) or Vanilla Biscuits dough (see page 36) if posting; makes 6 mummy ducks and 18 baby ducks

1 quantity Basic Royal Icing (see page 21)

line icing

primrose
baby pink
baby blue
bright yellow
black

flooding icing

primrose
baby blue
baby pink

All of the ducks are decorated in the same way.

Pipe on the beak with bright yellow line icing, then outline around the whole of the edge of the biscuit in either baby pink, baby blue or primrose yellow. Allow to dry for about 5 minutes. * Fill in the head and body area with the flooding icing that matches your chosen line colour. * If any air bubbles appear, pop them with the tip of a cocktail stick and gently tap the biscuit to even out the surface. Allow to set completely. * Ice on a ribbon and bow at the neck using line icing and then use black to make a little spot for the eye.

Baby Shower

This is such a sweet collection and it is beautifully simple to ice. We have used primrose yellow for all of the trimmings, but you can change that for baby pink or powder blue icing if you know what is expected!

cutters

baby vest
cube
bootie
pram
rattle
teddy

recipes

1 quantity of Vanilla Biscuits dough (see page 36); aim to make 24 biscuits

1 quantity Basic Royal Icing (see page 21)

line icing

white
primrose
donkey brown

flooding icing

white
teddy brown

rattle

Pipe outline in white line and leave to dry. * Fill with white flooding icing. Remove air bubbles. * Allow to dry briefly and then add little details in primrose line.

pram

Ice the wheel and spokes in brown line icing and the outline of the hood and pram in white. * Allow to dry and then flood with white runny icing. * Remove air bubbles. * When set, add details in primrose line icing to the hood and the sides of the pram. * Finish with a little lacy ruffle to the front of the hood in white line icing.

bootie

Ice on the knitted pattern just as with the baby vest, remembering to change the direction of icing to make the heel and toe. * Allow to set, then add the ribbon using primrose line.

teddy

Pipe outline of head, arms, legs, feet, muzzle and ears in brown line icing. * Leave to set then flood feet and muzzle with white and the rest of the body in brown runny icing. * Finally pipe the details of nose, eyes and ears in brown line.

cube

Ice all around the outside with primrose line. * Flood with white runny icing. * Allow to dry briefly, then add cube details and ABC with primrose.

baby vest

Using white line icing, pipe on 'knitted' texture to the whole of the vest. * Let this set, then add seam details and poppers in yellow line.

Birthday Party

This is one birthday party that we wouldn't mind planning. A Biscuiteers collection of nice things to have at your party that are bound to go down well. We have fallen in love with fondant fancies and wobbly jelly all over again...

cutters

balloon
square for battenburg
party hat
rectangle
circle for lollipop
fondant fancies
jelly
slice of cake

recipes

1 quantity Super Chocolatey Biscuits dough (see page 36); makes 14–16 biscuits

1 quantity Basic Royal Icing (see page 21)

line icing

primrose yellow
Aegean blue
white
raspberry
red
baby blue
violet

flooding icing

Aegean blue
primrose yellow
baby pink
raspberry
white

extras

lollipop stick

jelly

Outline the jelly in raspberry and the plate in white line icing and allow to dry. * Flood the jelly in raspberry and the plate in white runny icing and then immediately pipe on Aegean blue line icing details. * Leave to dry and then finally ice on the white line highlights.

fondant fancies

Choose any colour for your fancy. Ice line all around the outside and leave to dry. * Flood with runny icing of the same colour and allow to dry again. * Use the coloured line icing to add the shape of the cake and pipe on the 'icing' in white line.

candle cake

Outline the side of the cake in white line icing, the candle in baby blue line icing, the flame in primrose yellow line icing and the icing in raspberry line icing. * Allow all to dry and then flood all the areas with corresponding colours. Dry for 5 minutes. * Add dots and jam on the cake with pink, white and parma violet line icing. * Add stripes to candle and line the edge of the cake in baby blue. * Finish with white line dots to make the decoration on the cake.

presents

Choose your favourite colours then use the same method as for balloons to ice the present. * When it is dry, add a ribbon in fine line icing.

battenburg cake

Outline the square in white line icing and add another line just inside that to make the border. * Use yellow line icing to add a cross in the centre. Leave to set. * Flood the border with white flooding icing. * Allow to dry then flood alternate squares with pink and primrose yellow runny icing. * When this is dry add line detail with yellow over the cross in the centre.

balloon

Use any colour for your balloon. Outline the whole shape with coloured line icing and leave to set. * Flood but don't overfill with coloured runny icing and then immediately dot with little spots of white runny icing. * Add a white line knot when everything is dry if you like.

party hat

Use primrose line icing to outline the whole of the cone shape and also to add three stripes to the hat. * Allow to dry then flood the top and middle areas with Aegean blue icing. Leave to dry. * Flood primrose yellow icing in the other areas and leave to dry again. * Use primrose yellow line icing to add definition between the strips and white line to add the elastic.

lollipop

Outline in white line icing, dry for 5 minutes and then flood in runny white icing. * Before this sets add a spiral in raspberry line icing and drag a cocktail stick towards the centre to make the florentine pattern. * Dry and then add another spiral over the top in white.

Home Sweet Home

These houses are great to ice. We have chosen a tiny hamlet's worth here, but the possibilities are endless. They make a lovely house-warming or 'welcome home' gift and you can add your own and friends' houses to the collection too. Ice roses over the doors, geraniums in pots, pets peeping out of the windows and whatever little details turn them from houses into homes.

cutters

square
rectangle
(or cut freehand with a knife)

recipes

1 quantity Vanilla Biscuits dough (see page 36); number made depends on how big you want your houses to be

1 quantity Basic Royal Icing (see page 21)

line icing

white
black
grey
donkey brown
fuschia
red
raspberry

flooding icing

baby blue
teddy brown
white
lime green
grey

thatched cottage

Ice door and window outlines in white line icing. * Add thatch in brown line. * Outline cottage in white and allow to dry. * Flood with white. * Use line icing to add timber frame, chimney and door details and any other decorations.

fisherman's cottage

Pipe outline of slate roof in grey line. Add windows, wall lines and door details in white line and allow to dry. * Flood house in baby blue and roof in grey. Allow to set. * Add details in line icing. for windows, house name and cat (not pictured).

front door

Choose whichever colours you like. Outline whole door in coloured line and leave to dry. * Flood with chosen colour and allow to set. * Pipe on door panels, knocker and handle details in line icing.

town house

Pipe a white outline around windows and the blue wall area. Allow to dry. * Flood in baby blue. * When set, add details to windows in white line, and roof and door in raspberry pink line.

castle

Ice the outline of the turrets, walls, doors and windows in brown line and allow to dry. * Flood all of the stonework with grey or teddy brown runny icing. Allow to set. * Use line icing to add the stone, stairs and brick details. * Add the doors and final details in black line.

Cake Decorations

kit

baking parchment
nozzles
piping bags

recipes

1 quantity Basic Royal Icing
(see page 21)

line icing

choose your
favourite colours

flooding icing

choose your
favourite colours

embellishments

a little light glitter

There is more to baking than just biscuits. However, we find that the softer and more uneven texture of cakes makes icing the Biscuiteers way a little tricky. We make our own decorations by icing onto parchment or parchment/silicone sheets, allowing them to dry and then adding these to the top of cupcakes or birthday and wedding cakes.

If you are using parchment you can trace over your favourite designs with the icing. Whatever you choose to do, make sure that the lines are not too delicate as they will break on removal from the parchment, and that the little decorations are placed into a warm oven set to the lowest heat setting and totally dried before being peeled off the backing.

Any of our biscuit designs can be iced onto parchment. Take the sheets of parchment or silicone and place them on a baking sheet. Start with the outlines and ice in the normal way until you have as many decorations as you need. Little iced shapes are lovely for children's individual cakes. Try bumblebees, butterflies, ladybirds and flowers for pretty cakes. Or snails, snakes, lizards, beetles and frogs for more robust little Biscuiteers. When the shapes are all totally dry and have been peeled off the baking parchment you can use them like the shop-bought decorations. They will store for several weeks in an airtight tin as long as they are totally dry before being packed away. Layer them up between sheets of greaseproof paper to protect them and keep them from breaking.

You can make or buy cakes to decorate. Use buttercream icing as a base and press the decorations into this, or use line icing as 'glue' to stick the little shapes onto the sides and top of more formal cakes. Keep it simple…or go as mad as you like.

Wedding Day

This collection has all things bright and beautiful that you might find on that special day. We have chosen lime greens and hot coral pink but you can cut and ice to match the wedding day you have in mind. Bake for engagements, fabulous favours or thank yous for helpers on the day.

cutters

ballet shoes
topiary
fascinator
cake
cup
wedding dress

recipes

1 quantity Vanilla Biscuits dough (see page 36); makes 12–14 biscuits

1 quantity Basic Royal Icing (see page 21)

line icing

raspberry
parma violet
ivory
strawberry mousse
lime green
grape
black
white
pea green

flooding icing

white
parma violet
lime green
raspberry
orange
red

embellishments

gold lustre paint

bridesmaid's shoes

Outline the heel and peep toe in red line icing and the upper of the shoe in raspberry line icing. * Allow to set and then flood each area with red and raspberry runny icing. * When set pipe on raspberry line straps, white line toe details, dots and centre of flower. * Add parma violet line petals.

topiary flowers

Outline the stem in parma violet line icing, the pot and rim in lime green line icing and leave to dry. * Flood the pot with lime green, the soil in white and the stem in rarma violet runny icing. * When dry use raspberry, strawberry mousse and violet line icing to add flowers, pea green for the flower buds and white line dots in the centre of each flower.

fascinator

Outline the flowers and feathers in strawberry mousse line icing, leave to dry and then flood the petals with orange runny icing. * When set add fine black netting and more feathers in line icing, little lime green line leaves and parma violet flower centres. * Finally add white line detail to petals and feather tips.

cake

Pipe around the three layers of the cake in white line icing, leave to dry then flood with white runny icing. * Let this set then add lime green lines, raspberry, strawberry mousse and grape flowers all in line icing. * Add tiny white line centres and lime green leaves too. * Finally add a row of little white line dots to the base of each layer and brush with gold lustre paint when set.

wedding dress

Outline the skirt, bodice and sleeve details in white line icing and leave to set. * Flood the dress in white runny icing and burst any little bubbles that form with a cocktail stick. * Allow to set. * Add white line flowers decorations and dress pleats and little raspberry pink flowers.

cup and saucer

Outline the teacup, underside of saucer and handle in lime line icing. * Outline the top of the saucer, the rim of the cup and the band on the cup in ivory line icing. Allow it all to dry. * Flood the saucer and inside the rim in white runny icing and the band on the cup in raspberry. * When set flood the rest with runny lime green icing. * Dry then add flower detail in grape, lime and white line and detail around handle and on saucer in raspberry.

Wedding Favours

From little organza bags filled with pastel-coloured hearts, to place card biscuits with wedding guest names, there are so many reasons to ice biscuits for weddings. Here are some of our favourite designs.

We normally ice only in pale ivory and pastel shades, but the colours can be as bright as you like. And the favours can all be made totally personal. We have been asked to make baby rugby balls, pink elephants, top hats, motorbikes and ballet shoes. You can add initials or names and dates too.

Follow all the usual rules for icing and have a look at our packaging section (see pages 141–43) for inspiring ideas for wrapping them up.

Alphabet & Numbers

Say whatever you want with this simple-to-ice selection of letters and numbers. You can tell it how it is, spell out your messages of love, ice the initials of all your friends, say 'Thank you', 'I'm sorry', 'Get well soon' or '21 today'. Here are just a few ways to decorate your biscuits.

cutters

letters
numbers
(or cut rectangles and ice your letters and numbers onto them)

recipes

1 quantity Super Chocolatey Biscuits dough (see page 34) or Vanilla Biscuits dough (see page 36); number of biscuits will depend on size of cutters, makes approx. 20 x 5–7cm letters

1 quantity Basic Royal Icing (see page 21)

line icing

white
red
baby blue
gentian blue
welly green

flooding icing

Aegean blue
red
white
welly green

embellishments

only if you want to

polka dots

Ice around outside of your letter or number in line colour of your choice. Allow to dry for at least 5 minutes. * Flood middle with a contrasting colour, but don't overfill. * Ice on polka dots immediately with white line icing for a glossy finish.

stripy

Ice around outside in line colour of your choice. Allow to dry for at least 5 minutes. * Flood with a contrasting colour – try not to overfill. * Pipe the stripes immediately with white line icing for a glossy finish.

contrasts

Pipe around outside with line icing colour of your choice. Allow to dry for 5 minutes. Flood with a contrasting colour.

patchwork

Ice around outline in your chosen colour. Allow to dry for 5 minutes. * Flood with same colour – try not to overfill. * Pipe on polka dots in white immediately. Leave until set. * Ice 'stitches' around outside in a contrasting colour.

flag

Lots of flags have quite tricky patterns, so we use only line icing. * Print an image of your chosen flag and place your biscuit in the middle of it. (This will help you to recreate the pattern on the biscuit.)

Tips: Letter and number biscuits can be a little fragile, so if you need to post these biscuits perhaps just ice onto squares or rectangles. If you find it tricky to get the flooding icing into all the corners of the letter and number shapes, just push it around with a cocktail stick to exactly where it needs to be.

Cakes & Cupcakes

Like the treats in the window of the best cake shop in town, these glossy little cakes, buns and strawberry tarts look so tempting.

cutters

tart
éclair
circle (for buns and doughnuts)
cupcake

recipes

1 quantity orange flavoured Plain Biscuit dough (see page 33); makes 4 angel cakes, 4 cupcakes and 2 each of the other designs

1 quantity Basic Royal Icing (see page 21)

line icing

mustard yellow
baby pink
ivory
donkey brown
teddy brown
red
black
pea green

flooding icing

donkey brown
baby pink
red
teddy brown
ivory

embellishments

anything goes – hundreds and thousands, flowers, baubles or glitter

cupcakes

Make them up in your favourite colours or ice outline of cupcake case in ivory line icing. * Flood case with ivory. Allow to set. * Add donkey brown line details to case. * Squeeze flooding icing (without an outline) onto the top of the cake just as if you were icing a real cake. Allow to set. * Add iced decorations or other sprinkles.

chocolate and strawberry tarts

Ice outlines of the strawberries in red line and the tart case in donkey brown line. Allow to dry for 5 minutes. * Flood the strawberries with red and the base with teddy brown. Immediately add seed detail to strawberries with yellow line. Leave to set. Pipe lines on tart case in donkey brown.

doughnuts

Pipe outline of icing and hole in pink line. Allow to set. * Flood with pink. * When set add hundreds and thousands by piping tiny little lines onto the surface of the icing.

éclairs and choux buns

Ice around outline of éclair in ivory line. Add the outline of the chocolate with donkey brown line. Allow to dry for 5 minutes. * Flood the chocolate of the éclair with dark brown flooding icing and the pastry with teddy brown line icing. Rough light brown icing up with knife or spatula to make it look like choux pastry.

Cat & Mouse

These are the Biscuiteer cats. You can ice yours in any shade you like, or add your own kitty's favourite toy.

cutters

fish
goldfish bowl
mice
milk bottle
circle (for ball of wool)

recipes

1 quantity Super Chocolatey Biscuits dough (see page 34); makes about 16

1 quantity Basic Royal Icing (see page 21)

line icing

white
black
orange
grey
baby pink

flooding icing

black
orange
white

tom cat

Outline in black line and leave to dry for 5 minutes. * Put a little blob of white flooding icing on cheek and at tip of tail and ears if you wish. While still wet, fill rest of cat with black flooding icing. With tip of cocktail stick, 'feather' icings so they blend together. Leave to dry. * Add eye with white line icing and black line and nose in pink.

ball of wool

Ice strands of wool in line icing over and over until it looks like a ball of wool.

mouse

Outline in white. Allow to dry for 5 minutes. * Flood mouse in white. Leave to set. * Add tiny spot of black for eye, and nose and tail in baby pink.

goldfish bowl

Ice outline in white and flood with white. Allow to dry. * Pipe a goldfish in orange line, the rim of the bowl in black and the water line in white. * Add dot in black line for the fish's eye.

fish bones

Ice all of the fish bones using white line icing. * Add a black dot for the eye.

milk bottle

Ice around outline in black and allow to dry for 5 minutes. * Flood with white and allow to set. * Use black line to add details to neck of bottle and add 'MILK' across centre.

Best in Show

This is a sophisticated monochrome pack of pooches. There are lots of different dog cutters available and you can colour the icing to match your hound, or keep things simple like these fine examples from the Biscuiteers kennels. Pop some of the runny black icing into a piping bag to make adding details easier.

cutters

selection of dog cutters:
whippet
labrador
sausage dog
poodle
dalmatian
boxer
spaniel
jack russell
pekingese

recipes

1 quantity Vanilla Biscuits dough (see page 36); makes 12–16 depending on the hounds in your pack

1 quantity Basic Royal Icing (see page 21)

line icing

black
white

flooding icing

black
white

whippet, labrador and sausage dog

Pipe the outline of the dogs – legs, ears and tails in black line icing. * Leave to set then flood with runny black icing. * Leave to dry then add details of eyes, white tummies and ears using black and white line icing.

dalmatian and boxer

Outline the dogs in black line icing and leave to set. * Flood with white runny icing and then immediately add face and spot details with runny icing in a piping bag.

poodle

Outline the poodle in black line icing all around the body, legs and face. * Allow to set then flood with black runny icing. * When dry use plenty of white line to add pompoms to neck, feet and tail.

spaniel, jack russell, pekingese

Outline the dogs in white line icing and leave to set. * Flood bodies with white runny icing, but don't overfill. * Immediately add dots, spots and face details using black runny icing and a piping bag. * When dry use black and white line icing to add eyes and fur detail.

Catwalk Collection

We have chosen our own colour palette for this collection of favourite shoes and peacock feather earrings. But you can recreate this wardrobe to match your own if you wish. Sugar diamonds, gold lustre and glitter can be used to add highlights too if you like a little bling on your biscuits.

cutters

dress
glasses
wedge
strappy high heel
earring (use smallest
Russian doll outline)
watch
handbag
swimming costume

recipes

1 quantity Vanilla Biscuits
dough (see page 36); makes
14–16 biscuits depending
on the size of your gown

1 Basic Royal Icing (see page 21)

line icing

eucalyptus
grey
ivory
black
white
pea green
gentian blue

flooding icing

black
eucalyptus
white
ivory

embeliishments

gold lustre paint

peacock earrings

Pipe little circles in ivory line icing just touching each other for the feathers and one at the top for the jewel. * Leave to dry for 5 minutes. Flood with eucalyptus runny icing and leave to set. * Add ivory and black details all over in fine line icing.

swimming costume

Outline the costume in ivory and when it is dry fill with ivory runny icing. * Allow to dry and then add patterns and flowers in pea green, eucalyptus, ivory, black and grey line icing. * Finish by adding straps in fine ivory line icing.

dress

Ice an oval in black line icing at the neck and then add little wiggles of eucalyptus, black, white, grey and gentian blue all over the dress. * Allow to dry then flood the oval with black runny icing and finally add white highlights in line icing.

sunglasses

Outline the lenses in grey and allow to dry. * Fill with black flooding icing and leave until set. * Add little dotty flowers in grey, white and eucalyptus line, highlights to lenses in white line icing and hinges of glasses in grey line icing.

watch

Pipe a double border in grey line icing. * Pipe chain detail in grey and then leave to dry. * Flood watch face in white and border in grey runny icing. * When dry add numeral details to face and highlights to chain in white line icing.

handbag

Outline the bag and a line 1cm from the top and bottom in eucalyptus line icing. * When dry, fill the middle with eucalyptus, the bottom with grey and top with white runny icing. * Allow to dry then ice ivory wiggly lines over the grey area, black line icing between the sections and add the handles in eucalyptus line icing. * Add detail to the handles in ivory line icing and brush with gold lustre paint when dry.

strappy high heel

Outline the heel, sole and strap with eucalyptus line icing and when it is dry, flood with runny icing. * Use ivory line icing to add a triangle pattern on the heels whilst the flooding icing is still wet. * Allow everything to dry. * Pipe on toe section, shoe details and dots in ivory line. * When set finish with eucalyptus line icing around toe section.

Fashion Shoes

This is your chance to add six new pairs of shoes to your collection in one day. Bake these for your girlfriends, give them to your mother, send them to your sister, but don't expect the men in your life to understand the fascination.

cutters

knitted boots
party shoes
spike heels
wedges
sneakers

recipes

1 quantity Treacle Spice Biscuits dough (see page 39); makes approx. 14 biscuits depending on which pairs you make

1 quantity Basic Royal Icing (see page 21)

line icing

baby pink
rose
black
red
lime green
grape
white

flooding icing

baby pink
white
lime green
red

embellishments

coloured glitter sugar

wedges

Ice sole with grape line icing. * Use rose line icing to outline 'leather' area, including peep toe, strap and inside of shoe. Leave to dry for 5 minutes. * Flood 'leather' area with lime green. Allow to set. * Add buckles or flowers to front in your favourite bright line icing.

knitted boots

Ice on classic crêpe sole using black line icing. * Create 'knitted' texture in light rose line icing all the way up boots. Change angle of 'knitting' so it looks like the real thing. Allow this to dry briefly. * Use baby pink line to add heel details and black line to add the buttons.

party shoes

Pipe around outline and also top edge of shoe in bright line icing. Leave to dry for 5 minutes. * Flood soon-to-be sequinned area with white. Allow to dry for 1 minute. * Sprinkle with glitter sugar. Tap off excess once set. * Add bow or buckle of top seam detail in line icing.

spike heels

Pipe heel, sole and straps in grape line icing. Leave to set. * Fill in between lines of straps in white line icing. Add lime line to sole area and heel and allow to dry. * To add sparkle detail pipe tiny spots of white line icing down front of shoe and sprinkle with glitter while still wet. Tap off excess when icing is dry.

sneakers

Ice outline of red area in rose line icing. Use white line icing to add sole and tip of shoe. Leave to dry for 5 minutes. * Flood shoe with red. Allow to set. * Pipe on eyelets, sole detail and ventilation holes with fine black line. * Use white line to add logo background, seam details and laces. * Pipe on your initial or logo in grape.

Presents for the Teacher

These biscuits make a lovely present for anything to do with school. Say thank you to your child's teacher or send exam good luck wishes or congratulations for getting into university. If completing the whole collection looks a little complicated, just a selection of bright and beautiful drawing pencils looks lovely. Choose a pretty mug to pack them in for a luxury tea and biscuits gift!

cutters

apple
pencils
paper
blackboard
ruler
protractor
palette
school bus

recipes

1 quantity of the recipient's favourite biscuit dough; makes at least 16

1 quantity Basic Royal Icing (see page 21)

line icing

bright yellow
orange
red
gentian blue
welly green
donkey brown
white
black

flooding icing

bright yellow
red
orange
white
baby blue
black
welly green

paper

Ice around outline and holes in paper in white line and allow to dry for 5 minutes. * Flood whole page with white. Pop any little bubbles that appear with tip of a cocktail stick and tap biscuit to even out surface. * Before icing has chance to set add fine red line for margin and fine blue icing for lines on paper.

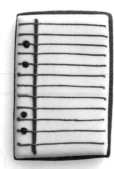

school bus

Ice around outline, windows, sign, headlights and mirror details in yellow line icing. Leave to dry for 5 minutes. * Flood body with yellow and the sign and headlights with white. Allow to set. * Add 'School Bus' lettering, bumpers, wipers and wheels in line icing.

apple

Pipe around outline of apple in red, remembering to include bite mark. Add stalk in brown and leaf outline in green. Leave to dry for 5 minutes. * Flood apple with red and the leaf with welly green.

ruler, protractor & palette

These three are all iced in the same way. Pipe white line icing all around the outside and let it dry for 5 minutes. * Flood whole shape with white icing and pop any air bubbles. Leave to set. * Use black line icing to add details.

pencil

Pipe black outline around pencil. Add a line where it has been sharpened to and pipe 'lead' of pencil in a bright colour. Leave to dry for 5 minutes. * Flood pencil with chosen colour and the wooden area with white. Leave to set. * Pipe detail on the pencil in black line.

blackboard

Use brown line icing to pipe border around edge of blackboard. Leave to dry for 5 minutes. * Flood rectangle with black icing. Leave to set. * Use white line and flooding icing to 'draw' on blackboard.

On Safari

We have rounded up all of our favourite animals for this safari collection, but you might like to add some more of your own.

cutters

mummy and baby elephant
butterfly
parrot
lion
tiger
giraffe
crocodile

recipes

1 quantity cinnamon-and-orange flavoured Plain Biscuit dough (see page 33); makes 14–16 biscuits

1 quantity Basic Royal Icing (see page 21)

line icing

grey
white
bright yellow
donkey brown
orange
red
fuschia
black
welly green

flooding icing

fuschia
welly green
orange
bright yellow
grey
donkey brown
baby blue
red
white

lion

Ice the mane in orange line icing using lots of little swirly movements. * Use yellow line to outline face and body. Allow to dry for 5 minutes. * Flood with yellow. Leave to set. * Add paws and leg details in yellow, an orange tip to the tail and a nose in donkey brown line.

parrot

Outline parrot in red line icing. Add lines between different colour areas in red line. Leave to set for 5 minutes. * Fill individual areas with flooding icing and allow to dry briefly. * Add feet, eye and beak details, and red line over-piping to wing and head.

rhino

Outline rhino body in grey. * Allow to set then flood with grey flooding icing. * When dry add horn, toe, eye and ear details in black and white line icing.

giraffe

Outline all around shape in bright yellow line icing. Leave to dry for 5 minutes. * Flood with yellow but don't overfill. Before yellow icing sets add markings in donkey brown line and allow to dry. * Add eye and tail in black and white line.

crocodile

Ice around outside of crocodile in welly green. Allow to dry for 5 minutes. * Flood with welly green. Leave to set. * Pipe teeth with white line, feet detail in brown line, eyes in black and white line and the pattern on skin in welly green line.

butterfly

These can be any colour you like. Pipe the body and wing outline in line icing. Allow to dry for 5 minutes. * Flood wings with same colour icing. Allow to set. * Add spots and patterns in lots of bright colours using flooding and line icing.

tiger

Outline tiger shape in black and allow to dry. * Add white flooding icing on belly, ears and muzzle then flood rest of body in orange flooding icing and leave to set. * Use line icing to pipe lots of black stripes and markings all over. * Add face details in black line.

mummy & baby elephant

Pipe grey line around elephant shape. Allow to dry for 5 minutes. * Flood with grey. Leave to dry briefly, then add tusks, eye and feet in white line. * Add ear detail in grey line and a black dot on the eye.

Biscuiteers circus

These bright and beautiful biscuits recreate the scene of an old-fashioned circus. We love their gaudy colours and are very proud of our clever seal and dancing elephant. Vary the palette if you like, but our Biscuiteers' circus always performs well in these vibrant colours.

cutters

ringmaster's coat
sea lion
elephant
sad clown
carriage
big top/sideshow booth

recipes

1 quantity orange flavoured Super Chocolatey Biscuits dough (see page 34); makes approx. 12 biscuits

1 quantity Basic Royal Icing (see page 21)

line icing

black
white
grey
red
bright yellow

flooding icing

orange
red
raspberry
grey
white
bright yellow

embellishments

gold and silver baubles

sad clown

Ice around outline in black line icing. Allow to dry for 5 minutes. * Flood whole clown in white. Burst any little bubbles in white icing with a cocktail stick. Leave to set. * Use black line to add all details and pattern to the clown's outfit. * Use red line icing to add mouth and tears.

sea lion

Ice around ball in red line icing and add segments in middle. * Use red line icing to pipe around stand in zigzag pattern. * Ice outline of sea lion in grey. Leave to dry for 5 minutes. * Add raspberry and white flooding icing to ball, flood sea lion with grey and stand with white and red. Allow to set. * Use line icing to add white dot on ball, white top and red dots on stand and a twinkly eye and wet nose in black.

elephant

Ice around elephant in grey line icing. Allow to dry for 5 minutes. * Flood elephant with grey and leave to set. * Use red line to outline ball and stripes across it, headdress and rug. Allow to set briefly then squeeze raspberry flooding icing into headdress, rug and stripe on ball. * Add yellow detail in line icing to feathers on headdress. * Flood ball with red.

carriage

Ice around outline, including wheels, in yellow line icing. Leave to set for 5 minutes. * Fill with red flooding icing and allow to dry briefly. * Add animal to the carriage (we used white line with black detail for our polar bear). * Use yellow line to add bars, decorations and details.

ringmaster's coat

Ice all black details, apart from bow tie and buttons, using black line icing. Allow to dry for 5 minutes. * Carefully use flooding icing to fill in red for coat, orange for waistcoat, bright yellow for collar and white for shirt. Leave to set. * Add the buttons and bow tie in black line icing.

big top/sideshow booths

Pipe on lines and fill in with red and white line icing. Allow to set. * Add carpet with red line and interior in black. * Add flag and banner details in line too.

Retro ski

This collection is packed with vintage ski kit at its best. Go off piste and ice it in your own favourite colours, or stick to our classic range.

cutters

scarf (use charity ribbon cutter)
skis (use pencil outline)
jumper
chalet (use beach hut outline)
bobble hat
mittens
ice skates

recipes

1 quantity treacle spiced dough (see page 39); makes 12–14 biscuits

1 quantity Basic Royal Icing (see page 21)

line icing

white
Aegean blue
gentian blue
donkey brown
red
black

flooding icing

red
white
grey
donkey brown
Aegean blue

scarf and jumper

These are both iced in the same way. Outline the garments in gentian blue line icing and allow to dry. * Flood with Aegean blue and leave to dry again. * Use red, white and gentian line icing to add pattern details.

mittens and bobble hat

Outline the mittens and the bobble hat in red line icing, leaving a little gap to add white fur trim, and leave to dry. * Flood the red areas and dry again. * Use white line icing to add fur trims and the bobble. * Add pattern to the hat using Aegean blue, gentian blue and white line icing. * And add straps to the mittens in red and black line icing.

ice skates

Outline the leather of the skate in white line icing, leave to dry and then flood in white runny icing. * Add the sole and heel in donkey brown line icing and outline the skate in grey. * When dry, flood the skate with grey runny icing and add eyelets in black and lace and shoe details in white.

chalet

Outline the wooden area and the window frames in donkey brown line icing and the snow with white line and leave to set. * Flood with runny brown and white icing and dry again. * Flood windows in gentian blue icing and when set add white line frames, balcony, chimney and steps.

skis

Outline both of the skis and the chevron shapes in black line and leave to dry. * Flood the centre with Aegean blue and the tips in red runny icing. * When set pipe on chevron and binding details in black and white line.

In the garden

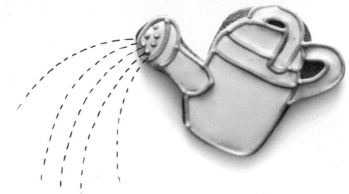

Everything is always perfect in the Biscuiteers' garden, just as long as we keep the creepy crawlies away from our lovely flowers and the vegetable patch.

cutters

wellies
tomato
carrot
watering can
spade
trowel
fork
leek
flowerpot

recipes

1 quantity orange flavoured Plain Biscuits dough (see page 33); makes at least 25

1 quantity Basic Royal Icing (see page 21)

line icing

welly green
primrose
teddy brown
red
black (tiny amount)
gentian blue
white
orange

flooding icing

welly green
teddy brown
red
orange
white
baby blue

watering can

Ice outline of can, spout and handle in gentian blue line icing and allow to set for 5 minutes. * Flood can with baby blue and leave to dry. * Over-pipe all lines and details on can in gentian blue line icing.

spade/trowel/fork

These are all iced in same way. Pipe all outlines of handles using brown line and shapes of tools using gentian blue line. Leave to dry for 5 minutes. * Fill the handles with brown flooding icing and the tools with baby blue. Let these set before adding any surface details with gentian blue line.

wellies

Pipe outline and heel in green line and leave to dry for 5 minutes. * Flood with green and allow to set. * Ice on ridges, seams and tie in green, label in red and white and buckle in black line.

flowerpot

Pipe outline in brown, including shape of rim. Use primrose, welly green and white line icing to add flowers and leaves. Leave to dry for 5 minutes. * Flood pot with runny teddy brown icing. * Add details in brown line.

carrot

Using line icing, pipe leaves at top in green and add a red outline around the outside. Leave to dry for 5 minutes. * Flood whole of carrot in orange and leave to set. * Add details in red line.

leek

Outline bottom of leek in white and leaves in green line icing. Allow to set. * Flood leaves with green and bottom of leek with white. Leave to set. * Pipe little roots in brown line and leaf details in green.

tomato

Ice outline in red. Leave to dry for 5 minutes. * Flood with red and leave to set. * Pipe on stalk in green.

Flower Power

These are brilliant biscuits for beginners. They can be as simple or as complicated as you like and you can use pretty much any colours you fancy. You can use flower-shaped biscuit cutters, plain and fluted round cutters or improvise by carefully pressing different-sized drinking glasses into your dough and cutting circles.

cutters

flowers or plain/fluted circles
leaf (see tip)

recipes

1 quantity Super Chocolatey
Biscuits dough (see page 34):
makes 20–24 biscuits

1 quantity Basic Royal Icing
(see page 21)

line icing

welly green
orange
bright yellow
raspberry
white
violet
deep-sea blue

flooding icing

welly green
parma violet
bright yellow
raspberry
orange
white
pink

embellishments

gold and silver baubles
silver glitter sugar

starburst flower

Use white line to ice a fat circle in the middle and fill centre with raspberry line. * Add petals in deep-sea blue line.

pink passion flower

Ice two circles in raspberry in centre of flower like a bullseye. * Flood centre with raspberry and outer ring with parma violet. * Ice petal shapes around outside in raspberry line. * Fill petals with pink flooding icing. Allow to dry for at least 2 minutes. * Use white line icing to make stamen pattern and then line ice around this in raspberry.

eggplant

Ice a line of touching dots around centre of the flower. Add spiky petals in raspberry line and allow to dry. * Flood centre in bright yellow flooding icing and add final spot details in green line.

Tip: We sometimes bake our biscuits spiked onto wooden secures. If you want to try this, use a lower temperature oven 130°C for 25 minutes so the sticks don't burn.

retro orange flower

Ice a white circle of dots in middle of biscuit and a stylised petal pattern around the outside of the flower. * Fill middle with yellow flooding icing and petals with orange runny icing. * Allow to dry. * Pipe on green centre, orange dots and green line pattern.

shamrock

Ice around outside in violet line. * Fill with violet flooding icing. Allow to dry. * Use yellow line to ice a ring of touching dots and fill inside with raspberry flooding icing. Allow to dry. * Decorate pink area with a circle of white line icing.

Tip: We make lovely little leaves to go with our flowers. You can buy leaf cutters or simply use an overlapping circle cutter to make the same shape. If you are making these biscuits for eagle-eyed children, try adding the odd bite to the leaves and a few little caterpillars to see if anyone notices.

Doll's House

Our Biscuiteers doll's house has fabulous food and sparkling furniture. Gold lustre is a thick gold edible paint that can be brushed onto the surface of biscuits to add a little glimmer of gold. Use a clean brush and a little paint to highlight the raised pattern on the furniture.

cutters

dressing table
grandfather clock
round
rectangle
house
clothes peg dolls

recipes

1 quantity Vanilla Biscuits dough (see page 36); makes 1 large house, 2 dolls and 6–8 accessories

1 quantity Basic Royal Icing (see page 21)

line icing

ivory
donkey brown
black
red
rose
fuchsia
eucalyptus
baby pink
Aegean blue
white
pea green

flooding icing

ivory
donkey brown
white
baby pink
baby blue

him

Outline face, neck, arms and legs in white line, the shirt in Aegean blue line icing and shorts in donkey brown line icing. * Allow to set and then flood corresponding areas in ivory, baby blue and donkey brown runny icing. * Add shirt pattern in Aegean blue line icing and use baby pink flooding icing for the cheeks whilst the runny icing is wet and then leave everything to dry. * Pipe shirt detail in Aegean blue line icing and then the shorts, braces and eyes in donkey brown, cuffs and buttons in white and hair and braces detail in ivory line icing.

her

Outline face, neck, arms and legs in white line icing and the dress in baby pink line icing. Allow to dry. * Flood the dress in baby pink icing and use fuchsia and ivory line icing to add pattern straight onto the wet icing. * Allow to dry then flood the legs, arms and face with ivory runny icing. * Add baby pink cheeks this is still wet. * When dry add black hair and eyes, white cuffs, pink line dress pleats and fuchsia bow all in line icing.

plates of food

Ice the plate with white line border, leave to dry and then flood with white runny icing. * Add pattern to the plate when still wet then leave to dry again before adding your favourite food in line icing.

doll's house

Pipe the outlines of the windows and door frame in Aegean blue line icing. * Add a donkey brown and white icing outline to the roof, walls and chimney pot and leave it to dry. * Flood the roof in white and the walls in brown runny icing. * When set add white line bricks, window frames and door. * Use pea green line icing for the roof tiles and red line to add porch. * Finally paint gold lustre onto the door handle.

dressing table and grandfather clock

These are both iced in the same way. Use ivory line icing to outline all the way around the dressing table, stool and clock and add heart and mirror shape to the dressing table and panel in the grandfather clock too. Allow to dry. * Flood all of the ivory areas in runny icing and the panel and mirror in baby blue. * When dry add pattern, mirror supports, numbers and decorations in ivory line icing. * Pipe white line reflection onto mirror and paint gold lustre onto the raised pattern with a fine brush.

Great British Summer

We do like to be beside the seaside at Biscuiteers. So we made this very vintage collection with all the British beaches that we have ever been to in mind. Add your own fish and chips, windbreaks, beachballs and gritty picnics or whatever it is that sums up a day at the beach for you.

cutters

starfish
kite
seagull
bikini
ice cream
bucket & spade
beach hut

recipes

1 quantity Simple Butter Biscuits dough (see page 37) or Super Chocolatey dough (see page 34); makes 14-18 biscuits
1 quantity Basic Royal Icing (see page 21)

line icing

bright yellow
orange
red
white
gentian blue
black
pea green
donkey brown

flooding icing

orange
bright yellow
red
white
gentian blue
pea green

embellishments

use demerara sugar or brown glitter sugar for the sand and candy strands for the ice cream

kite

Ice the quarters of the kite and the string for the tail in yellow line icing. * Allow to set then flood quarters in yellow and gentian blue. * Leave these to set then add the tail's coloured bows in line icing.

polka dot bikini

Use red line to ice outline of the bikini. * Leave to set then flood with runny red icing until just full. * Add spots of white runny icing before the red has set.

seagull

Use line icing all over in black and white to make the seagull's body and feathers. * Allow to dry then finish with bright orange beak and a little black dot for the eye.

beach hut

This is iced in line icing only. Start with the white outline of the shape of the beach hut and door. * Then fill in all the stripes first in pea green and then in white. * Allow to set fully then use white line icing to ice on the area of sand at the front. * Sprinkle immediately with demerara sugar and allow to dry. * Add a little plaque for your beach hut name and a black line door handle. * When these have set ice on your name in black line.

ice cream

Use donkey brown line to ice the waffle of the cones. * Leave to set then use coloured line icing thickly applied for the balls of ice cream in your favourite flavour and a chocolate flake in donkey brown line. * Sprinkle on the candy strands before the icing has set.

starfish

Outline and flood in orange, green or yellow. * Allow to dry then add spot and eye details in black and white line icing.

bucket

Outline in yellow line adding rim and corner details to the bucket. Leave to dry. * Flood all over with yellow runny icing. Leave to set. * Add a spot more runny icing where you want the sand and dust with demerara sugar. * When dry add the bucket handle detail in white line.

spade

Outline in yellow line and leave to dry. * Flood with runny yellow icing and sprinkle the demerara sugar on the spade tip for sand. * Leave to dry.

Tropical Fish

Bright and bold, this aquarium of fish and friends looks lovely against the rich chocolate brown biscuits. You can make simpler versions, and use fewer colours if you like, but we love this all out explosion of the colours of the reef.

cutters

assorted fish
seaweed
crab
lobster
starfish
anemone

recipes

1 quantity Super Chocolatey Biscuits dough (see page 36); makes 14–16 biscuits

1 quantity Basic Royal Icing (see page 21)

line icing

strawberry mousse
raspberry
orange
white
Aegean blue
eucalyptus
bright yellow
pea green
black

flooding icing

orange
Aegean blue
strawberry mousse
black
pea green
raspberry
white
fuchsia
bright yellow

sea anemone

Ice round tentacles in raspberry line icing and the base in white line icing and leave to dry. * Flood with corresponding colours and dry again. * Pipe on line and dot details in white and raspberry line icing.

rainbow fish

Using line icing outline the body in orange and add fins in raspberry and Aegean blue. * When set flood the body with red, raspberry, orange and white runny icing. * Squeeze on a colour at a time and do not overfill. * Add a black eye using runny icing and stripes of Aegean blue last and leave everything to dry.

striped fish

Outline fish and bottom fin in Aegean blue and add strawberry mousse and Aegean fronds to fins all in line icing. * When dry flood the body and fin sparingly with Aegean blue, add stripes of strawberry mousse and the black and white eye detail all in runny ice. * Leave to dry. * Finally pipe tiny dot details in strawberry mousse and Aegean blue line icing.

crab

Pipe shell and claw outline in strawberry mousse line icing, allow to dry then flood with runny strawberry mousse icing. * Before it sets add eucalyptus, Aegean blue and black runny icing pattern to shell. * When all dry add strawberry mousse line detail to pincers, pipe legs and add black and white line eyes.

coral and seaweed

Ice around the outline of each in pea green or orange, leave to set and then flood with corresponding colours. * When dry use orange and pea green line icing to add little circle details.

yellow and green fish

Outline body and fins in bright yellow line icing, leave to set then flood sparingly with orange runny icing. * When still wet add green and fuchsia runny icing pattern and a black eye then leave to dry. * Finish with line spot and fin detail.

starfish

Outline starfish in strawberry mousse line icing and allow to dry. * Flood with a little white runny icing and immediately add strawberry mousse runny icing pattern. * When dry pipe tiny raspberry line dots to add details.

lobster

Pipe outline in orange line icing, dry and then flood in runny orange icing. * Add strawberry mousse line chevrons on back immediately and dry again. * Add orange line legs, tentacles and shell details and black and white eye balls.

Hot Wheels

There are heaps of car cutters available so look out for your own wheels and paint them to match or make some of our classic cars. Vary the colours, numbers and stripes of your ride as you wish.

cutters

triangle (cut freehand)
traffic light (use cricket bat)
Fiat 500
Mini
motorbike
key (use smallest Russian doll)
Beetle
campervan

recipes

1 quantity Vanilla Biscuits dough (see page 36); makes 12–14 cars and accessories

1 quantity Basic Royal Icing (see page 21)

line icing

black
grey
bright yellow
red
raspberry
gentian blue

flooding icing

black
grey
bright yellow
grey
red
raspberry
Aegean blue
orange
ivory
pea green

key

Outline the fob in black line icing and the metal in grey line icing and when dry fill with corresponding colours. * Leave to set then add the details in grey and black line icing.

motorbike

Outline the whole of the body of the bike in bright yellow line icing and then outline all the black areas and the grey exhaust in line icing. * Allow everything to dry and then fill in the black, yellow and grey areas with flooding icing. Leave to dry completely. * Add detail to body with black line icing. * Pipe on the forks, chassis and spokes with grey line icing and pick out exhaust details too.

danger sign

Outline, dry and then flood the whole triangle in red. * Wait for 5 minutes before outlining, drying and flooding the inner triangle in white. * When this is dry a pipe black line icing exclamation mark.

Fiat 500

Outline car body, roof and window area in red line icing. * Allow to dry then flood with red runny icing. * Pipe inner and outer circles of tyres in black line icing and leave to set. * Flood tyres with black runny icing and windows with grey runny icing. * Use line icing in red, black and grey to add bumper, hub cap, trim and lights.

Beetle

Ice the Beetle in the same order as the Fiat 500. * Use raspberry icing in place of red.

campervan

Outline the base of the campervan body in gentian blue line icing and the top of the cab and rest of body in white line icing. * Add windows in white line and allow to dry. * Flood the base in Aegean blue runny icing, the top of the cab in white and the rest in ivory. * Outline wheels in black line icing and when dry flood windows and wheels with grey runny icing and add trim details in black line icing.

traffic light

Pipe white line icing in a double border around top of the traffic light. * Outline the pole and round lights in black line and allow to dry. * Flood the lights in red, orange and green runny icing, the pole in grey and the frame in white. * Leave to set. Flood around the lights in black.

London

This is home ground for Biscuiteers. We have cherry-picked our favourite London icons and iced them just for you. Add a few of your own landmarks too. Buildings are particularly good as you can just ice them onto easy-to-cut squares and rectangles.

cutters

circle (for Tube sign)
telephone box
London Bridge
postbox
Big Ben
oval (for London Eye)
taxi

recipes

1 quantity Super Chocolatey Biscuits dough (see page 34); makes at least 15 biscuits

1 quantity Basic Royal Icing (see page 21)

line icing

bright yellow
black
white
red
donkey brown
teddy brown
grey

flooding icing

black
red
white
grey
teddy brown
gentian blue

Tube sign

Ice yellow line around rectangular nameplate and outer circle. Ice around inner circle in white. Allow to dry for 5 minutes. * Flood nameplate in blue, inner circle in white and outer circle in red. Leave to set. * Pipe name in black.

taxi

Pipe outline of bodywork and windows in black line, leaving space to ice on wheels later. Leave to dry for 5 minutes. * Flood with black. * Add wheels in black line icing. Leave to set. * Fill windows and add a radiator with grey line icing. Use line icing to add all other details.

telephone box

Pipe all red line details and pipe base outline in black. Allow to dry for 5 minutes. * Flood top of box with red and base with black. Flood light at top with white. (Leave windows uniced.)

postbox

Ice top of box in red line and base in black line and lines in between. * When dry flood top with red and base with black. Allow to dry. * Use red, black and white line icings to add details.

Big Ben

Outline whole shape in white line and leave to set. * Flood with white runny icing and, when dry, use light and donkey brown and grey line icing to add bricks and clock face.

London Bridge

Look carefully at a picture of the bridge before you ice it. Use donkey brown line to add all outlines for stone sections, including line down centre of each pillar that divides teddy brown and white flooding icing. Leave a gap for walkway. Leave to dry for about 5 minutes. Flood base of pillars and left-hand side in teddy brown and right in white. Allow to dry. * Use brown line to add detail to pillars. * Add all blue and white line details that make up remainder of bridge.

London Eye

Use white line icing to pipe frame and wheel. * Add spokes and inner frame in grey line. * Ice tiny capsules in black and grey line icing.

Paris

This is our take on the capital of sophistication: Paris. We've included a dainty Parisian poodle and all her favourite landmarks.

cutters

Eiffel Tower
Arc de Triomphe
Notre Dame
name plaque
poodle
boulangerie

recipes

1 quantity Super Chocolatey Biscuits dough (see page 34); makes at least 15, add poodles from trimmings

1 quantity Basic Royal Icing (see page 21)

line icing

Aegean blue
grey
leaf green
white
light baby pink
baby pink
red
black

flooding icing

white
Aegean blue
baby pink
gentian blue
grey

Eiffel Tower

Ice blue outline around triangle. Add rows of grass at base with green line icing. Allow to set for 5 minutes. * Flood background in Aegean blue. Before this sets, add little clouds in white flooding icing. Let this dry for 2 minutes. * Ice structure in black line.

poodle

Pipe around outline in baby pink line and allow to dry for 5 minutes. * Flood whole of the dog with light baby pink icing and leave to set. * Add nose and bow details in black and pink line.

name plaque

Ice around shape in grey. Add outline of name and district plaques in blue line. Leave to set. * Flood around plaque with grey. Fill in plaque with Aegean blue. Allow to set. * Add text in grey and white, detail lines in white and the little grey line embellishments.

boulangerie

Use Aegean blue line to ice around top area of shop, door and windows. Use red line to ice along bottom of shop front. Leave to dry for 5 minutes. * Flood sides and shop sign with white. Leave to set. * Add flowers, door handle, door detail and 'BOULANGERIE' using appropriate coloured line. * Our boulangerie is a mini work of art; make yours a little simpler if you wish.

Arc de Triomphe/ Notre Dame

For the Arc de Triomphe ice outline of arc in grey line and edge of biscuit in blue line. Allow to dry for 5 minutes. * Flood appropriate areas with white and Aegean blue flooding icing. Leave to set. * Use grey line to add stone details to arch. * Decorate Notre Dame biscuit in same way, but without sky background.

baking & icing   123

New York

There are quite a few colours to mix for this collection, but the icing is relatively straightforward. We have chosen our best bits from the city that never sleeps. You can add you own street names, bridges, bagels or whatever else that will make it your take on New York.

cutters

hot dog
taxi
road signs
skyscraper
Statue of Liberty
apple

recipes

1 quantity Super Chocolatey Biscuits dough (see pae 34); makes at least 15 biscuits, make extra hot dogs or 'I heart New York' stickers with any trimmings

1 quantity Basic Royal Icing (see page 21)

line icing

white
grey
black
red
bright yellow
eucalyptus
donkey brown

flooding icing

welly green
ivory
grey
donkey brown
eucalyptus
mustard yellow
red

taxi

Pipe outline of taxi and its windows using yellow line. Don't forget to leave space for wheels. Leave to dry for 5 minutes. * Flood taxi with yellow. Allow to dry briefly. * Pipe black line inside windows, on bumper and tyres. * Add the details in line icing: chrome trim on hubcaps, bumper and windows in grey; white line on numberplate and bumper; brake lights in red; 'NYC', 'AXI' and round circle for 'T' in black; 'T' in yellow.

big apple

Ice outline of apple in red. Allow to dry for 5 minutes. * Flood with red. Leave to dry. * Pipe in 'I' and 'NY' in black line, add white heart and stalk in black line icing.

hot dog

Ice outline of wiener in donkey brown and the bun in white. Allow to dry for 5 minutes. * Flood wiener with donkey brown and the bun with ivory. Leave to set. * Add ketchup and mustard wiggles in red and yellow line icing.

road signs

Outline sign in white and allow to dry for 5 minutes. * Flood with green and leave to dry. * Pipe on street name in white line.

skyscraper

Outline in grey and allow to dry. * Flood with grey and leave to dry. * Pipe all windows, doors and details using grey line icing.

Statue of Liberty

Ice all of outline, except the flame, using eucalyptus line. Allow to dry. * Flood with eucalyptus. Leave to set. * Add all details in eucalyptus green line. * Ice flame in yellow line and add details to crown in grey line.

Biscuit Classics

Here we have a seriously delicious Biscuiteers version of biscuit tin classics. We find that they are too precious and tasty to even consider dunking in our tea.

butter cream recipe

100g butter

200g icing sugar

Beat these together with your chosen flavouring ingredients until light and fluffy and completely combined. Keep the butter cream covered closely with clingfilm until you are ready to use it so that it doesn't begin to go hard before you use it.

flavouring butter cream

Vanilla

add a couple of drops of vanilla essence

Chocolate

1–2 dessertspoons of sieved cocoa powder

Lemon or orange

add the finely grated zest of 2 oranges or lemons

Coffee

add 1 teaspoon of instant coffee

Custard creams

1 quantity Vanilla Biscuits dough (see page 36)

1 quantity vanilla butter cream

1 quantity Basic Royal Icing (see page 21) made into ivory-coloured icing (see page 23)

1 piping bag

Cut by hand, or use a rectangular cutter to make 24 Vanilla Biscuits. * Cook and cool as per instructions. * Use the line icing to pipe on the details and name to the 12 tops of the biscuit in the traditional custard cream pattern. * Use a palette knife to spread butter cream onto the 12 base biscuits. * Press the iced biscuit tops down onto the butter cream until they are stuck together.

Iced gems

Make these from leftover scraps of dough or icing. Cut and bake a tiny circle and top with icing squeezed through a star nozzle (see page 31 for picture).

Linzer biscuits

1 quantity Simple Butter Biscuits dough (see page 37)

1 quantity of vanilla butter cream

5 tablespoons of your favourite jam

1 round crinkly edged cutter

mini cutters for the centre

Cut 24 circles with the larger cutter. * Take half and use the smaller cutters to cut out a little hole in the centre * Bake as usual. * When the biscuits are totally cool take the 12 base biscuits and pipe a thick ring of icing around all the outside edges of the biscuit to make a wall to hold in the jam. * Then spoon a little of your favourite jam into the centre of the biscuit and spread evenly inside the icing ring. * Squash the top down onto the base until they are firmly stuck together.

Bourbons

1 quantity Super Chocolatey Biscuits dough (see page 34)

1 quantity chocolate butter cream

1 piping bag of donkey brown icing

Hand cut or use a rectangular cutter to make 24 Super Chocolatey Biscuits. * Use the prongs on a fork to spike little lines of dots all down the biscuits. * Cook and cool as per instructions. * Then pipe the name onto the biscuits with the line icing. * Sandwich the biscuits together with a big squidge of chocolate butter cream.

Make Oreo Cookies using a similar method, but cut rounds, fill with vanilla buttercream and pipe on the distinctive Oreo pattern in the donkey brown icing.

Party ring

1 quantity Vanilla Biscuits dough (see page 36)

1 quantity Basic Royal Icing (see page 21), made into 3 colours of flooding icing and pink line icing

1 piping bag

1 large and 1 small round cutter

Use the two cutters to make the ring biscuits. Bake and cool as per instructions. * Pipe on the outline in line icing around the edge and centre. * Squeeze on the runny flooding icing inside the lines and add spots and lines of different colours. * Feather the icing using the tip of a cocktail stick.

Creepy Crawlies

We love these creatures. You can make them as friendly or as fierce as you like. We used to make a spider, but it was a little too close to the real thing to be truly enjoyable to eat. These biscuits are great for party bags and work well when personalised with initials or names. Stick to the cuter crawlies for younger biscuit eaters.

cutters

ladybird
caterpillar
snail
dragonfly
leaf
frog
lizard

recipes

1 quantity Treacle Spice Biscuits dough (see page 36); makes 2 of each creature

1 quantity Basic Royal Icing (see page 21)

line icing

lime green
baby pink
eucalyptus
leaf green
bright yellow
red
black
white

flooding icing

lime green
leaf green
baby pink
baby blue
red
black
bright yellow

embellishments

purple sparkly glitter sugar

ladybird

Ice head using black line icing. * Ice outline of shell in red line icing and allow to dry for at least 5 minutes. * Fill shell with red flooding icing (don't overfill). Immediately add spots of black flooding icing. Leave to set. * Add legs, antennae and line down back of shell in black line icing.

caterpillar

Outline shape with leaf green line icing. Allow to dry for 5 minutes. * Flood middle with lime green and leave to set. * Add segments to body using leaf green line. * Ice on legs, eyes and antennae in black line.

snail

Ice around outline of body in baby pink. Leave to dry for 5 minutes. * Fill with baby pink flooding icing. * Shell design is made with flooding icing straight onto biscuit without any line 'walls'. Start in middle and swirl icing around. Leave to set. * Add antennae and eyes in black line.

leaf

Ice around outside of leaf and stalk in lime green line icing. Don't forget to add a few little munch marks around edge. Allow the line to dry. * Fill leaf with leaf green flooding icing. Leave to set. * Ice on vein details in lime green line.

dragonfly

Ice body, head and outline of wings in eucalyptus. Leave to dry for about 5 minutes. * Fill wings with baby blue flooding icing. Allow to set for a minute then sprinkle on purple sparkly glitter sugar. Leave to dry. * Add legs in black line icing.

lizard

Ice all over using leaf green line icing, leaving two small areas for eyes. Allow to dry briefly. Add stripes in bright yellow line. * Pipe eyes in black and white line icing.

frog

Ice outline of frog in leaf green line icing and allow to set. * Flood body and legs with leaf green runny icing until just full then add tiny bright yellow spots in more flooding icing. Leave to dry. * Ice on eyes in black and white line icing.

Cowboys & Indians

These old-fashioned cowboys and Indians biscuits appeal to boys of all ages. Cacti have never tasted so good. If you have enough dough, make a whole village of tepees and ice them all differently.

cutters

cactus
tepee
horse
Stetson
boots
headdress

recipes

1 quantity orange flavoured Super Chocolatey Biscuits (see page 34) dough; makes 2 pairs of boots, 4 cacti, 1 horse, 1 headdress, 1 Stetson, 1 tepee, 5 arrows, 1 revolver

1 quantity Basic Royal Icing (see page 21)

line icing

welly green
sage green
lime green
ivory (make it dark)
red
black
gentian blue
bright yellow
donkey brown
white

flooding icing

welly green
donkey brown
sage green
ivory (make it dark)

tepee

Ice outline in donkey brown line and allow to dry for 5 minutes. * Flood with ivory and let dry until surface is hard. * Add wooden poles at top in black line. * Ice patterns in red, yellow and blue line.

boots

Ice around outline of boot in donkey brown. Allow to dry for 5 minutes. * Flood with ivory. Allow to set. * Ice the seams with brown line icing. Add the heel with lines of brown and the stitching detail in white.

horse

Ice around outside with dark ivory line. Allow to dry for 5 minutes. * Flood with ivory and allow to set. * Using line icing add saddle in multicolours and tail in brown. * Ice on hooves and eye and ear details in brown line.

cactus

Outline in welly green line and leave to dry for 5 minutes. * Fill with welly green flooding icing and allow to dry. * Add lines or spines in lime green line icing.

headdress

Made using only line icing. Use white to pipe on headband and white parts of feathers. * Add red and welly green tips to feathers and use yellow for feather quills.

Stetson

Ice around outline in donkey brown. Allow to dry for 5 minutes. * Flood with sage green and allow to set.

Pirate Party

These work beautifully as favours for pirate parties. Ice your own little pirates in their favourite T-shirts amongst this bloodthirsty crew.

cutters

cutlass
pirate ship
pirate
palm tree
treasure chest
skull and crossbones

recipes

1 quantity of your little pirate's favourite dough; makes 14–18 biscuits

1 quantity Basic Royal Icing (see page 21)

line icing

red
white
black
Aegean blue
leaf green
mustard yellow
orange
donkey brown

flooding icing

red
white
black
donkey brown
leaf green

embellishments

gold and silver glitter sugar

pirate

Ice one area at a time. Use black outline to pipe around hat, hook, hand, stump and foot. Leave to dry for 2 minutes. * Flood hat with black. * Pipe white outline of shirt and red outline of shorts, leaving a gap for a belt in between. Allow to dry. * Flood shirt in white and shorts in red. Leave to set. * Pipe on big bushy orange beard in line icing. Add face and ears in white line. * Ice on details of belt, grin, eyepatch, eye, hat and stripes on the shirt. Ice the first mate in different combinations!

pirate ship

Outline hull and forecastle in brown line, remembering to add castle-like details. * Outline sail in white line and add stripes across it. Allow to dry. * Flood hull and castle with brown. Add red and white stripes to sail with flooding icing. Leave to set. * Pipe on castle bricks, stripes and portholes on the hull. Add a Jolly Roger in black and white line icing and an anchor in yellow and black.

treasure chest

Use brown line icing to pipe all outlines of the trunk. Make sure that it looks open and has space for some booty! Allow to set. * Flood the outside of the trunk with brown. Let this set completely. * Pipe the treasure area with yellow and let it set for a minute before adding golden glitter. * Add bands, lock and handles in yellow line icing.

skull and crossbones

Outline detail of the skull in black line. Remember to add face details. Leave to set. Flood skull and bones with white icing. * Pop any little bubbles below the surface with a cocktail stick.

palm tree

Ice outline of trunk in brown and outlines of leaves in leaf green. Leave to dry for 5 minutes. * Flood trunk in brown and leaves in green. Allow to set. * Add details of trunk, leaves and coconuts in brown and green line.

cutlass

Outline blade in white line icing and pipe grip in yellow. Allow to dry. * Flood cutlass blade with white. Let dry for 1 minute and then sprinkle on silver glitter.

Toy Box

These toys are all our favourites and we're sure you won't mind tidying them away. You don't have to make them all – you can mix and match.

cutters

xylophone
racing car
Russian dolls
train
plane

recipes

1 quantity Simple Butter Biscuits dough (see page 37); makes approx. 17 biscuits

1 quantity Basic Royal Icing (see page 21)

line icing

bright yellow
orange
leaf green
Aegean blue
red
donkey brown
baby pink
white

flooding icing

bright yellow
orange
leaf green
Aegean blue
red
white

embellishments

silver baubles

racing car

Ice outline and filling of tyres in red. * Choose your own car colour then ice around body in line icing and leave to dry. * Fill with coloured flooding icing and allow to set. * Add a little circle of yellow flooding icing to side of car. When set add number detail and steering wheel.

xylophone

Ice outline of bars with different coloured line icing. Allow to dry for 5 minutes. * Fill with corresponding flooding icing. * Add detail and beaters in brown line icing. Use a little silver bauble for end of beater if you wish.

plane

Outline each section of the plane in different coloured line icing. Allow to dry then flood each area with the same colour flooding icing. Add plane details with line icing.

train

Ice all outlines and borders of coloured areas in red line icing. Allow to dry for 5 minutes. * Fill in blocks of colour using flooding icing and leave to set briefly. * Add details of windows and lines down the engine's tank.

Russian dolls

Using five different colours, pipe on oval face on each doll in line icing. Add outline of dolls' bodies and allow to set. * Squeeze on flooding icing for each colour of doll and leave to dry. * Add details of eyes, cheeks, buttons, lips, noses and curls and any pattern to the dolls' bodies.

Little Girl's Fairy Party

Don't expect anyone over the age of ten to actually want
to eat more than a couple of the totally glittery biscuits.
The first pair of glitter shoes that we iced are framed
and still look fab after about five years.

cutters

ring
party shoes
wand
wings
tiara
butterfly
tutu

recipes

1 quantity Vanilla Biscuits dough
(see page 36) (good if biscuits
need to travel), or try Simple
Butter biscuits dough (see page
37) (not as sweet); makes about
15 biscuits, make lots of rings
with trimmings

1 quantity Basic Royal Icing
(see page 21)

line icing

baby pink
parma violet
white

flooding icing

white
baby pink
parma violet

embellishments

sugar crystals
(in different colours)
coloured baubles
(basically anything goes!)

party shoes

Ice the outline of the shoe, heel and
strap in baby pink line icing. * Leave to
dry then flood centre of shoe in pink
and sprinkle with coloured glitter.

butterfly

Pipe the whole of the wings in fine lacy
white line pattern. Sprinkle with silver
glitter. * When dry add pink details to
outside of wings and body.

wand & wings

Ice whole of wand and wing shape in
white and baby pink icing, including any
patterns, in white line icing. Immediately
add silver sprinkle glitter. Tap off any
excess when dry. * Add baubles using
a little white line icing as glue.

tiara

Use same method for tiara as for the
wand and wings. However, ice all pink
glitter areas first and add pink glitter.
* Allow this to dry totally before icing
more pattern with parma violet and
decorating this with purple glitter.

tutu

Start by icing all of the tutu outline
in parma violet line. Leave to set then
flood with parma violet runny icing.
Add little sugar crystals and leave to
set. * Pipe on frill at hem in line icing
and add pink dot and belt background.
finally add pink dot details to belt and
cover in pink sugar crystals.

Tip: Glitter only sticks to wet icing.
Make sure that all the background
areas are totally dry before you add
icing to the areas where you want
to stick your glitter.

Bake with Mother

Most children can ice some simple lines onto the biscuits and no children we know can resist trying lots of the icing. Choose how much they want to be involved with the preparation depending on their age. For tiny tots squeezing a few final lines of icing is probably where to start, but older children can normally manage to take on the whole biscuit. For when time is short, buy and store in the cupboard ready to use tubes of royal icing, available in white and several colours for impromptu icing on rainy days. There are several other collections in the book that are good for minis to ice too: they include Flower Power, Alphabet & Numbers, Christmas Baubles and the Iced gem biscuits.

cutters

ducks
dinosaurs

recipes

1 quantity dough of your
choice makes approx.
24 little ducks and
16 dinosaurs

1 quantity Basic Royal Icing
(see page 21)

line icing

white
bright yellow

flooding icing

white

embellishments

sparkly glitter sugar
shiny coloured baubles
favourite sweets to make
duck jewellery

ducks

Choose your favourite colours to ice
these little rubber ducks. Decide with
your little Biscuiteers age group in mind
if you want to ice the whole of the body
of the duck and let it dry so they can
add all the little details, sparkles and
baubles, or if they want to get totally
involved in the process. (See page
71 for icing instructions.)

dinosaurs

These are really simple to ice.
Using plain white line icing,
pipe on little bones and teeth
in all the right places. Add glitter
and sugars if you like too.

Other Ideas...

old chocolate boxes

For tiny biscuits you can use empty chocolate boxes with all their packaging. Cover the outside in wrapping paper or stickers and pop a tiny biscuit into each chocolate's space.

handmade envelopes

Using your biscuit as a guide for size, cut out an envelope shape that will cover the biscuit when all four corners are folded over. Place the biscuit inside and seal the top with a sticker or tie with ribbon.

favours and little biscuits

Organza or cellophane bags look lovely packed with little biscuits. Place mini biscuits inside and tie the top with ribbon.

cupcake cases

Stand three or four biscuits in a cupcake case and tie them together with a pretty ribbon and bow.

cellophane wrapping paper

Stand the biscuits carefully next to each other in a long line on a sheet of cellophane, then roll up the sides and tie up the ends like a cracker with pretty ribbon or twine.

cones of paper

Make little wrapping-paper cones and either fold over the top or make a little hole and thread with ribbon. These are really lovely for hanging from a Christmas or Easter tree.

biscuit card

Ice your biscuits in the usual way and draw round the outside of them on the front of a plain card. Draw some background details around your biscuit – flowers around a butterfly, huge leaves for dinosaurs, smart fences and a garden for a new house. Then pipe a little line icing onto the card inside the outline and press the biscuit down onto it to 'glue' it to the paper. Allow it to dry lying down and then pop it into an envelope.

Templates

how to make and use a template

You can ice a biscuit to look like pretty much any shape. If you are designing your own biscuits just remember that you can ice on much more detail than needs to be reflected in the shape of the biscuit. Also bear in mind that anything too delicate will often break at some point during the baking, cooking, icing or travelling process.

Included in this section are our favourite Biscuiteers bespoke cutters. To use them, simply place parchment paper over the pages and draw the outline in pencil over the shapes. If you think you will use the shape lots transfer the outline to thick clean card (a cereal box is useful) and cut out the shape. Then use the point of a sharp knife (a scalpel available from craft shops is really good but very sharp) to cut round the template on the dough. Alternatively, place the traced outline over your dough and use the tip of a satay or cocktail stick in place of a pen to impress a line through the parchment onto the rolled surface. Then cut round the marks using a sharp knife as above.

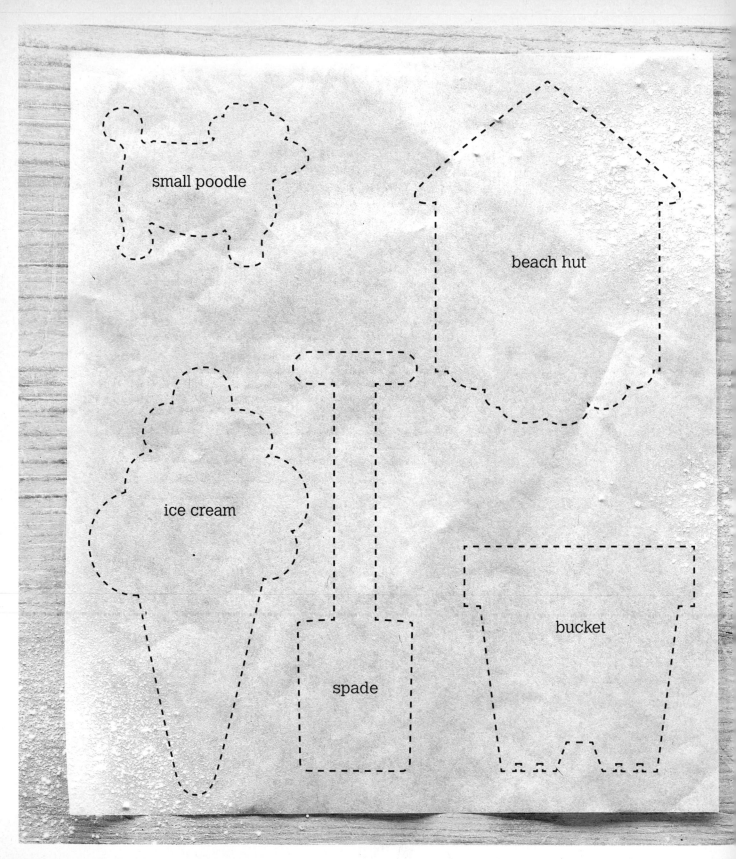

small poodle

beach hut

ice cream

spade

bucket

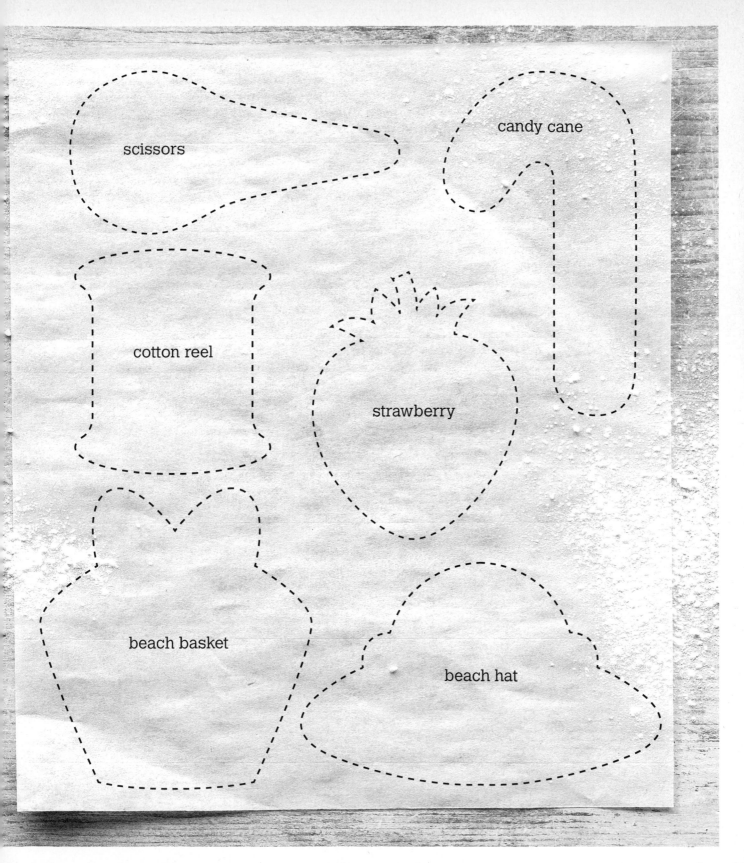

scissors

candy cane

cotton reel

strawberry

beach basket

beach hat

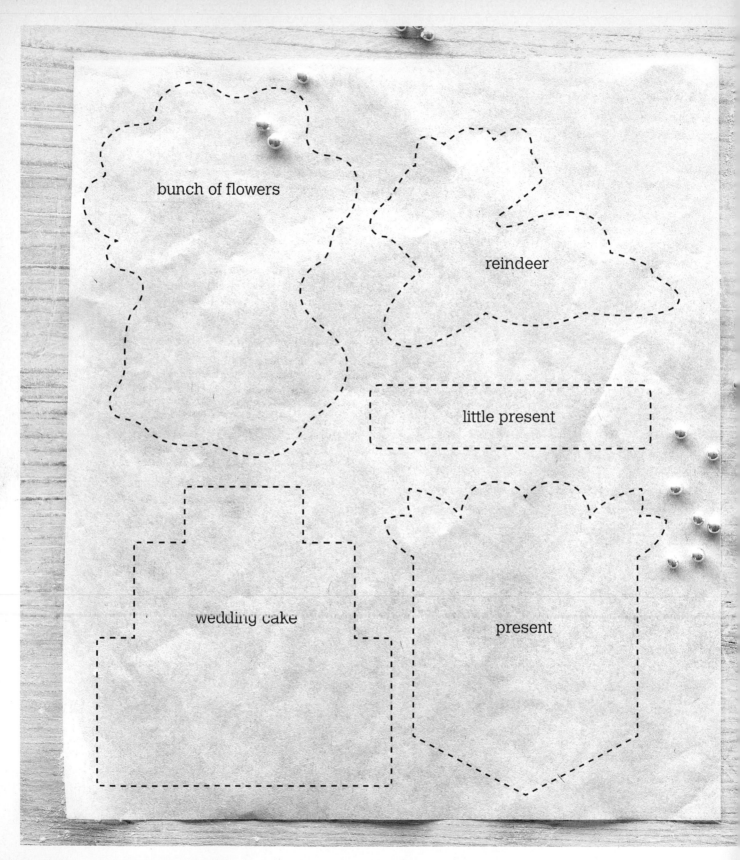

bunch of flowers

reindeer

little present

wedding cake

present

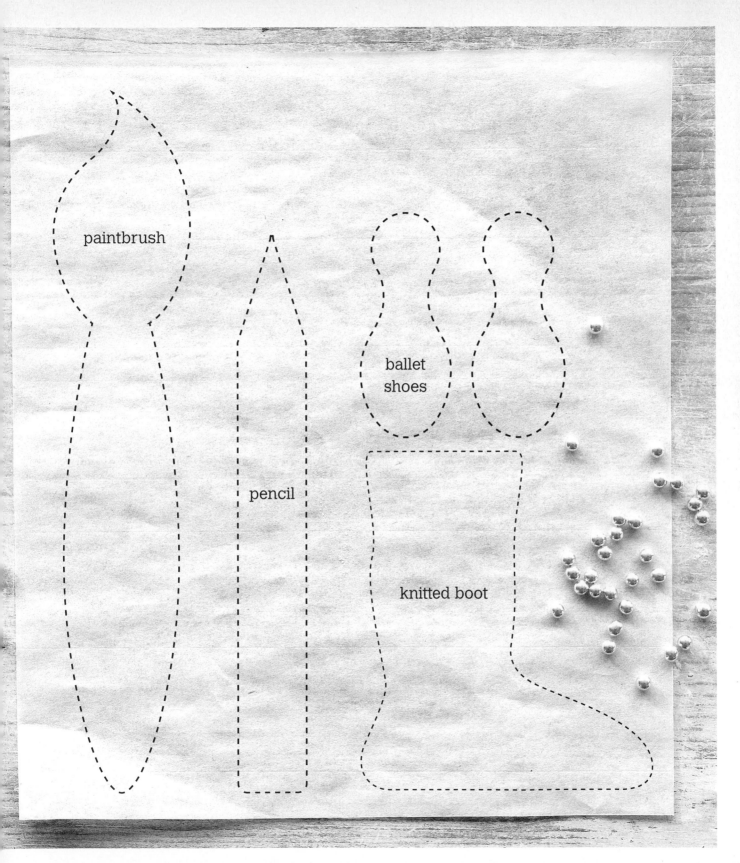

paintbrush

pencil

ballet
shoes

knitted boot

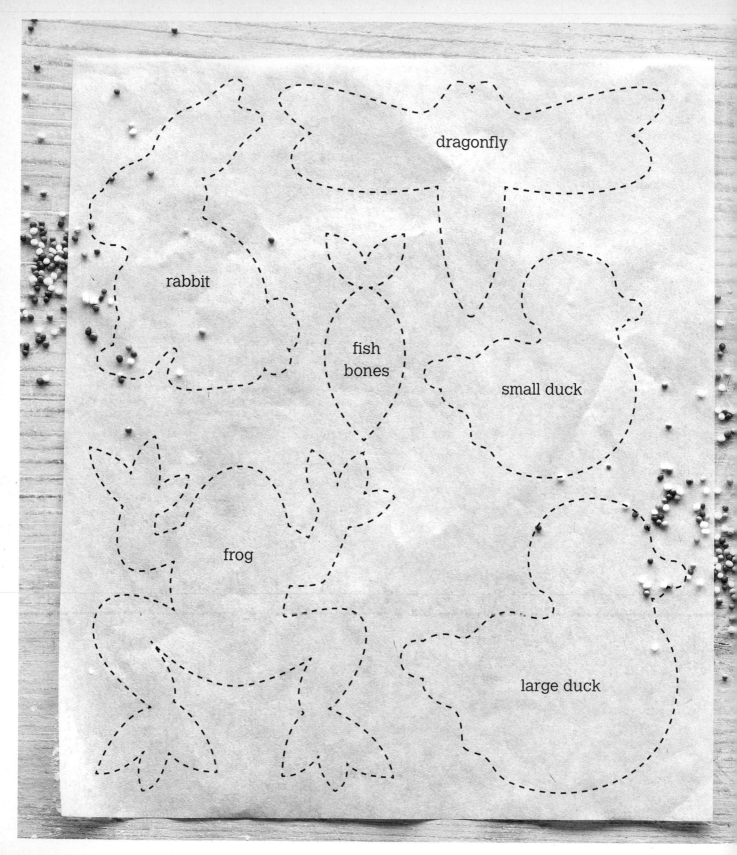

dragonfly

rabbit

fish
bones

small duck

frog

large duck

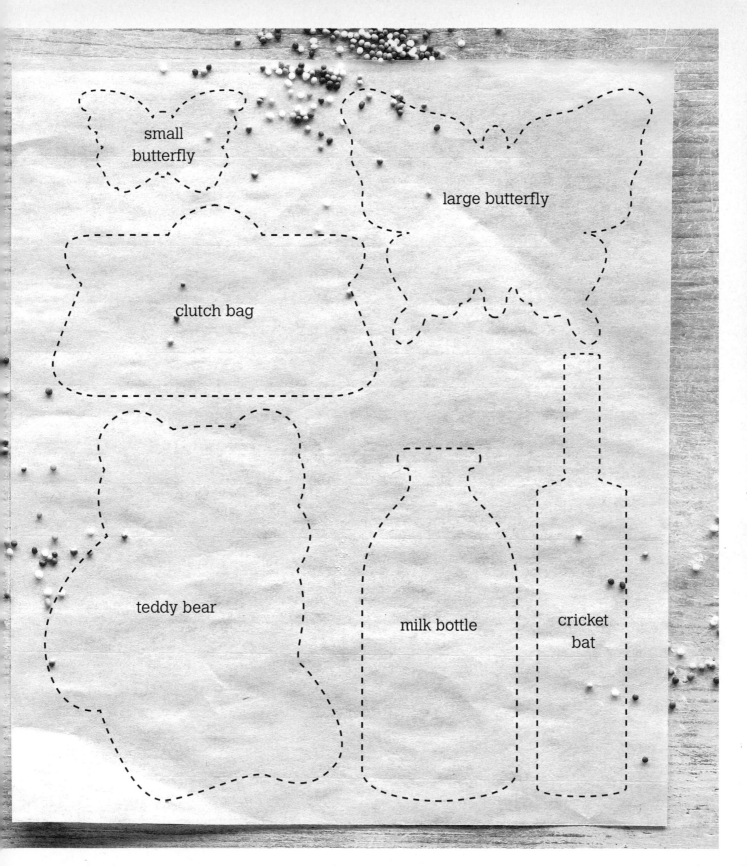

small butterfly

large butterfly

clutch bag

teddy bear

milk bottle

cricket bat

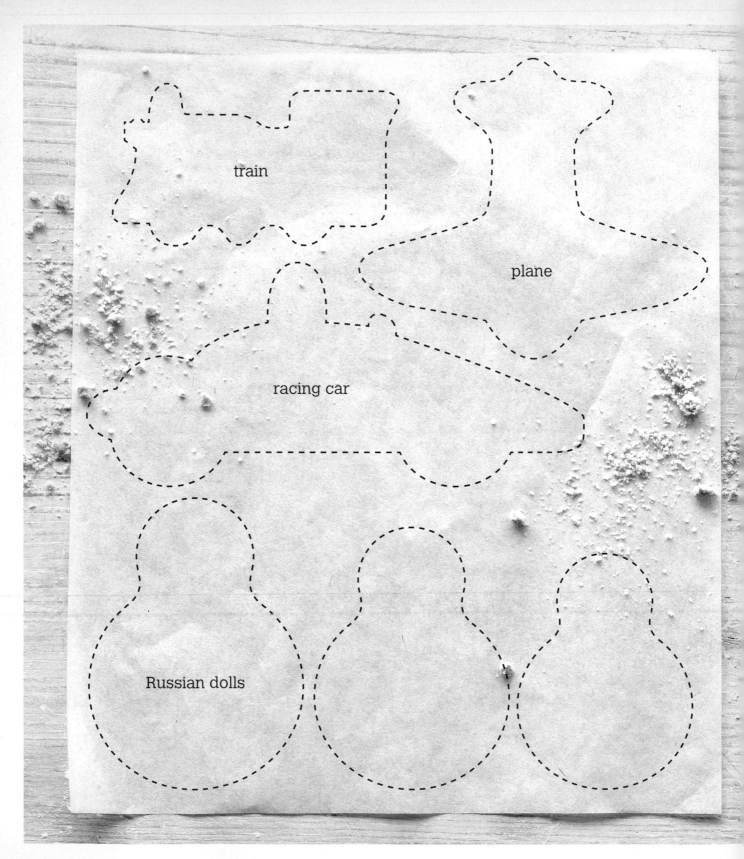

train

plane

racing car

Russian dolls

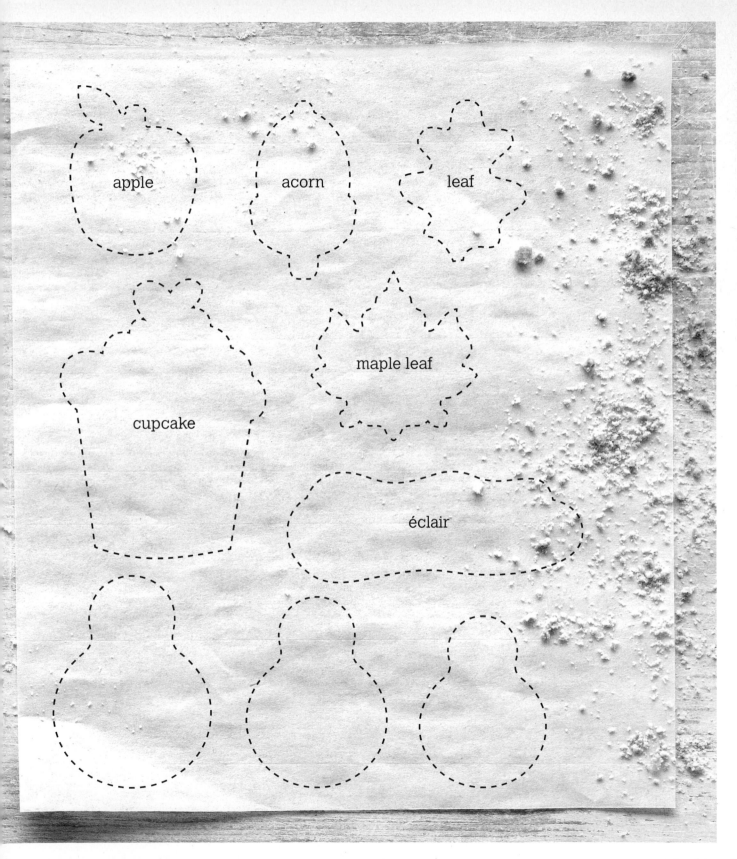

apple

acorn

leaf

cupcake

maple leaf

éclair

Suppliers

General ingredients:

Waitrose: www.waitrose.com – lots of baking ingredients, icing ingredients, baubles and cooking kit.

Ocado: www.ocado.com – home delivery for all sorts of useful cooking and baking ingredients.

Sainsbury's: www.sainsburys.co.uk – lots of baking ingredients, icing ingredients, baubles and cooking kit.

Tesco: www.tesco.com – baking ingredients, icing ingredients and some cooking kit.

The following shops supply cookie cutters, sprinkles and baking equipment:

Cookies, Cakes & crafts: www.cakescookiesandcraftsshop.co.uk – friendly and helpful business with more biscuit cutters than you can imagine and all the specialist ingredients, colours, sprinkles and baubles you could possibly want.

Jane Asher: www.jane-asher.co.uk – not just cakes: ingredients and equipment too.

The Cake Craft Shop: www.cakecraftshop.co.uk – good for all your biscuit needs too.

Sweet Success: www.sweetsuccess.uk.com

The Cake Place: www.thecakeplace.co.uk

Lakeland: www.lakeland.co.uk – all round good gadgets and helpful baking equipment.

Divertimenti: www.divertimenti.co.uk – specialist cooking shop with excellent range of professional cookware and equipment.

Squires Kitchen: www.squires-shop.com – the place to go for EVERYTHING for icing, decorating, colouring and shimmering.

Blends Limited: www.blendsltd.co.uk – for flavourings and colourings.

Woods: www.woodsfoodservice.co.uk – for colourings and vanilla pods in large quantities.

Overseal: www.overseal.com – these amazing people make natural and naturally derived colours from everything from black carrots to spinach. Available in large quantities only.

Two Chicks: www.twochicks.co.uk – really useful liquid egg available from supermarkets and independent retailers.

Biscuiteers Stockists:

UK
Harrods
Selfridges – London, Birmingham, Manchester
Liberty
Fortnum and Mason
Harvey Nichols
Fenwicks Newcastle

FRANCE
Colette
Le Grande Épicerie
Galeries Lafayettes

GREECE
Amadeus

DUBAI
Candylicious

Index

£5off

In addition to making the delicious
biscuits in this book, to purchase a
tin of Biscuiteers biscuits with a £5
discount off your first tin log on to
www.biscuiteers.com
and enter 'iceyourown' in
the discount code box.